THE HIGH SCHOOL FAILURES

A STUDY OF THE SCHOOL RECORDS OF PUPILS FAILING IN ACADEMIC OR COMMERCIAL HIGH SCHOOL SUBJECTS

By
FRANCIS P. OBRIEN, PH.D.

TEACHERS COLLEGE, COLUMBIA UNIVERSITY
CONTRIBUTIONS TO EDUCATION, NO. 102

PUBLISHED BY
Teachers College, Columbia University
NEW YORK CITY
1919

Library of Congress Cataloging in Publication Data

OBrien, Francis Paul, 1885-
    The high school failures.

    Reprint of the 1919 ed., issued in series: Teachers
College, Columbia University. Contributions to edu-
cation, no. 102.
        Originally presented as the author's thesis, Columbia.
    Includes bibliographies.
        1. Underachievers. 2. Academic achievement.
3. High school dropouts. I. Title. II. Series:
Columbia University. Teachers College. Contributions
to education, no. 102.
LC3965.O27 1972   373.1'28   70-177127
ISBN 0-404-55102-5

Reprinted by Special Arrangement with Teachers
College Press, New York, New York

From the edition of 1919 , New York
First AMS edition published in 1972
Manufactured in the United States

AMS PRESS, INC.
NEW YORK, N. Y.   10003

PREFACE

Grateful acknowledgment is due the principals of each of the high schools whose records are included in this study, for the courteous and helpful attitude which they and their assistants manifested in the work of securing the data. Thanks are due Dr. John S. Tildsley for his generous permission to consult the records in each or any of the New York City high schools. But the fullest appreciation is felt and acknowledged for the ready criticism and encouragement received from Professor Thomas H. Briggs and Professor George D. Strayer at each stage from the inception to the completion of this study.

F. P. O.

CONTENTS

A STUDY OF THE SCHOOL RECORDS OF THE PUPILS FAILING IN ACADEMIC OR COMMERCIAL HIGH SCHOOL SUBJECTS

CHAPTER I

GENERAL INTRODUCTION OF THE SUBJECT

1. The Relevance of This Study

As the measuring of the achievements of the public schools has become a distinctive feature of the more recent activities in the educational field, the failure in expected accomplishment by the school, and its proficiency in turning out a negative product, have been forced upon our attention rather emphatically. The striking growth in the number of school surveys, measuring scales, questionnaires, and standardized tests, together with many significant school experiments and readjustments, bears testimony of our evident demand for a closer diagnosis of the practices and conditions which are no longer accepted with complacency.

The American people have expressed their faith in a scheme of universal democratic education, and have committed themselves to the support of the free public high school. They have been liberal in their financing and strong in their faith regarding this enterprise, so typically American, to a degree that a secondary education may no longer be regarded as a luxury or a heritage of the rich. No longer may the field be treated as either optional or exclusive. The statutes of several of our states now expressly or impliedly extend their compulsory attendance requirements beyond the elementary years of school. Many, too, are the lines of more desirable employment for young people which demand or give preference to graduates of a high school. At the same time there has been no decline in the importance of high school graduation for entering the learned or professional pursuits. Accordingly, it seems highly probable that, with such

1

an extended and authoritative sphere of influence, a stricter business accounting will be exacted of the public high school, as the great after-war burdens make the public less willing to depend on faith in financing so great an experiment. They will ask, ever more insistently, for facts as to the expenditures, the finished product, the internal adjustments, and the waste product of our secondary schools. Such inquiries will indeed seem, justifiable.

It is estimated that the public high schools had 84 per cent of all the pupils (above 1,500,000) enrolled in the secondary schools of the United States in 1916.[1] The majority of these pupils are lost from school—whatever the cause—before the completion of their courses; and, again, the majority of those who do graduate have on graduation ended their school days. Consequently, it becomes more and more evident how momentous is the influence of the public high school in conditioning the life activities and opportunities of our youthful citizens who have entered its doors. Before being entitled to be considered a " big business enterprise,"[2] it seems imperative that our " American High School " must rapidly come to utilize more of business methods of accounting and of efficiency, so as to recognize the tremendous waste product of our educational machinery.

The aim of this study is to trace as carefully and completely as may be the facts relative to that major portion of our high school population, the pupils who fail in their school subjects, and to note something of the significance of these findings. If we are to proceed wisely in reference to the failing pupils in the high school, it is admittedly of importance that such procedure should be based on a definite knowledge of the facts. The value of such a study will in turn be conditioned by the scrupulous care and scientific accuracy in the securing and handling of the facts. It is believed that the causes of and the remedies for failure are necessarily closely linked with factors found in the school and with the school experiences of failing pupils, so that the problem cannot be solved by merely labeling such pupils as the unfit. There is no attempt in this study to treat all failures as in any single category. The causes of the failures are not assumed at the start nor given the place of chief emphasis, but are regarded as incidental to and dependent upon what the evidence itself discloses. The success of the failing pupils after they leave the high school is not included in this undertaking, but is itself a field worthy of extended study. Even our knowledge of what later happens to the more successful and the graduating high school pupils is limited mainly to those who go on to college or to other higher institutions. One of the more familiar attempts to evaluate the later influence of the high school illustrates the fallacy of overlooking the process of selection involved, and of treating its influence in conjunction with the training as though it were the result of school training alone.[3]

2. The Meaning of 'Failure' in This Study

The term 'failure' is employed in this study to signify the non-passing of a pupil in any semester-subject of his school work. The school decision is not questioned in the matter of a recorded failure. And although it is usually understood to negate "ability plus accomplishment," it may, and undoubtedly does, at times imply other meanings, such as a punitive mark, a teacher's prejudice, or a deferred judgment. The mark may at times tell more about the teacher who gave it than about the pupil who received it. These peculiarities of the individual teacher or pupil are pretty well compensated for by the large number of teachers and of pupils involved. The decisive factor in this matter is that the school refuses to grant credit for the work pursued. The failure for a semester seems to be a more adaptable unit in this connection than the subject-failure for a year. However, it necessitates the treatment of the subject-failure for a year as equivalent to a failure for each of the two semesters. Two of the schools involved in this study (comprising about 11 per cent of the pupils) recorded grades only at the end of the year. It is quite probable that the marking by semesters would actually have increased the number of failures in these schools, as there are many teachers who confess that they are less willing to make a pupil repeat a year than a semester.

By employing this unit of failure, the failures in the different subjects are regarded as comparable. Since only the academic and commercial subjects are considered, and since they are almost uniformly scheduled for four or five hours a week, the failures will seem to be of something near equal gravity and to represent a similar amount of non-performance or of unsatisfactory results. There were also a few failures included here for those subjects which had only three hours a week credit, mainly in the commercial subjects. But failures were unnoted when the subject was listed for less than three hours a week.

There are certain other elements of assumption in the treatment of the failures, which seemed to be unavoidable. They are, first, that failure in any subject is the same fact for boys and for girls; second, that failures in different years of work or with different teachers are equivalent; third, that failures in elective and in required subjects are of the same gravity. It was found practically impossible to differentiate required and elective subjects, however desirable it would have been, for the subjects that are theoretically elective often are in fact virtually required, the electives of one course are required in another, and on many of the records consulted neither the courses nor the electives are clearly designated.

3. The Scope and Content of the Field Covered

As any intensive study must almost necessarily be limited in its scope, so this one comprises for its purposes the high school records for 6,141 pupils belonging to eight different high schools located in New York and New Jersey. For two of these schools the records for all the pupils that entered are included here for five successive years, and for their full period in high school. In two other schools the records of all pupils that entered for four successive years were secured. In four of the schools the records of all pupils who entered in February and September of one year constituted the number studied. There is apparently no reason to believe that a longer period of years would be more representative of the facts for at least three of these four schools, in view of the situation that they had for years enjoyed a continuity of administration and that they possess a well-established organization. The fourth one of these schools had less complete records than were desired, but even in that the one year was representative of the other years' records. The distribution of the 6,141 pupils by schools and by years of entering high school is given below.

HIGH SCHOOL PUPILS IN:	ENTERING HIGH SCHOOL IN THE YEARS	NUMBER STUDIED
White Plains, N. Y.	1908, '09, '10, '11, '12	659
Dunkirk, N. Y.	1909, '10, '11, '12	370
Mount Vernon, N. Y.	1912	224
Montclair, N. J.	1908, '09, '10, '11, '12	946
Hackensack, N. J.	1909, '10, '11, '12	736
Elizabeth, N. J.	1912	333
Morris H. S.—Bronx	1912	1712
Erasmus Hall H. S.—Brooklyn	1912	1161
	TOTAL	6141

As it is essential for the purposes of this study to have the complete record of the pupils for their full time in the high school, the 6,141 pupils include none who entered later than 1912. Thus all were allowed at least five and one-half or six years in which to terminate their individual high school history, of successes or of failures, before the time of making this inquiry into their records. 'No pupils who were transferred from another high school or who did not start with the class as beginning high school students were included among those studied. Post-graduate records were not considered, neither was any attempt made to trace the record of drop-outs who entered other schools. Manifestly the percentage of graduation would be higher in any school if the recruits from other schools and the drop-backs from other classes in the school were included.

No attempt has been made to trace the elementary school or college records of the failing pupils, for our purpose does not reach beyond the sphere of the high school records. In reference to the differentiation by school courses, some facts were at first collected, but these were later discarded, as the courses represent no standardization in terminology or content, and they promised to give nothing of definite value. As might be expected, the schools lacked agreement or uniformity in the number of courses offered. One school had no commercial classes, as that work was assigned to a separate school; another school offered only typewriting and stenography of the commercial subjects; a third had placed rather slight emphasis on the commercial subjects until recently. Only four of the schools had pupils in Greek. The Spanish classes outnumbered the Greek both by schools and by enrollment. In the classification by subjects, English is made to include (in addition to the usual subjects of that name) grammar, literature, and business English. Mathematics includes all subjects of that class except commercial arithmetic, which is treated as a commercial subject, and shop-mathematics, which is classed as non-academic. Industrial history, and 'political and social science' are regarded along with academic subjects; likewise household chemistry is included with the science classification. Economics is treated as a commercial subject. At least a dozen other subjects, not classified as academic or commercial, including also spelling and penmanship, were taken by a portion of these pupils, but the records for these subjects do not enter this study in determining the successful and failing grades or the sizes of schedule. Yet it is true that such subjects do demand time and work from those pupils.

4. SOURCES OF THE DATA EMPLOYED

The only records employed in this whole problem of research were the official school records. No questionnaires were used, and no statements of pupils or opinions of teachers as such were sought. The facts are the most authoritative and dependable available, and are the very same upon which the administrative procedure of the school relative to the pupil is mainly dependent. The individual, cumulative records for the pupils provided the chief source of the facts secured. These school records, as might be expected, varied considerably as to the form, the size, the simplicity in stating facts, and the method of filing; but they were quite similar in the facts recorded, as well as in the completeness and care with which the records were compiled. It may be added that only schools having such records were included in the investigation.

After the meanings of symbols and devices and the methods of recording the facts had been fully explained and carefully studied for the records of any school, the selection of the pupil records was then made, on the basis of the year of the pupils' entrance to the school, including all the pupils who had actually entered and undertaken work. (Pupils who registered but failed to take up school work were entirely disregarded.) These individual records were classified into the failing and the non-failing divisions, then into graduating and non-graduating groups, with the boys and girls differentiated throughout. As fast as the records were read and interpreted into the terms required they were transcribed, with the pupils' names, by the author himself, to large sheets (16 x 20) from which the tabulations were later made. There was always an opportunity to ask questions and to make appeals for information either to the principal himself or to the secretary in charge of the records. This tended to reduce greatly the danger of mistakes other than those of chance error. The task of transcribing the data was both tedious and prolonged. This process alone required as much as four weeks for each of the larger schools, and without the continued and courteous coöperation of the principals and their assistants it would have been altogether impossible in that time.

Some arbitrary decisions and classifications proved necessary in reference to certain facts involved in the data employed in this study. All statements of age will be understood as applying to within the nearest half year; that is, fifteen years of age will mean within the period from fourteen years and a half to fifteen years and a half. The classification in the following pages by school years or semesters (half-years) is dependent upon the time of entrance into school. In this sense, a pupil who entered either in September or in February is regarded as a first semester pupil, however the school classes are named. As promotions are on a subject basis in each of the schools there is no attempt to classify later by promotions, but the time-in-school basis is retained. In reference to school marks or grades, letters are here employed, although four of the eight schools employ percentage grading. Whether the passing mark is 60, as in some of the schools, or 70, as in others, the letter C is used to represent one-third of the distance from the failing mark to 100 per cent; B is used to represent the next third of the distance; and A is used to express the upper third of the distance. The plus and minus signs, attached to the gradings in three of the schools, are disregarded for the purposes of this study, except that when D+ occurred as a conditional passing mark it was treated as a C. Otherwise D has been used to signify a failing grade in a subject, which means that the grade is somewhere below the passing mark. The term 'graduates' is meant to include all who graduate, either by diploma or by certificate. Any statement made in the following pages of 'time in school' or of time spent for 'securing graduation' will not include as a part of such period a semester in which the pupil is absent all or nearly all of the time, as in the case of absence due to illness.

5. THE SELECTION AND RELIABILITY OF THESE SOURCES OF DATA

By employing data secured only from official school records and in the manner stated, this study has been limited to those schools that provide the cumulative pupil records, with continuity and completeness, for a sufficient period of years. Some schools had to be eliminated from consideration for our purposes because the cumulative records covered too brief a period of years. In other schools administrative changes had broken the continuity of the records, making them difficult to interpret or undependable for this study. The shortage of clerical help was the reason given in one school for completing only the records of the graduates. In addition to the requirements pertaining to records, only publicly administered and co-educational schools have been included among those whose records are used. It was also considered important to have schools representing the large as well as the small city on the list of those studied. Since many schools do not possess these important records, or do not recognize their value, it is quite probable that the conditions prescribed here tended to a selection of schools superior in reference to systematic procedure, definite standards, and stable organization, as compared to those in general which lack adequate records.

The reliability and correctness of these records for the schools named are vouched for and verbally certified by the principals as the most dependable and in large part the only information of its kind in the possession of the schools. In each of these schools the principals have capable assistants who are charged with the keeping of the records, although they are aided at times by teachers or pupils who work under direction. In three of the larger schools a special secretary has full charge of the records, and is even expected to make suggestions for revisions and improvements of the forms and methods. In view of such facts it seems doubtful that one could anywhere find more dependable school records of this sort. It was true of one of the schools that the records previous to 1909 proved to be unreliable. There is no inclination here to deny the existence of defects and limitations to these records, but the intimate acquaintance resulting from close inquiry, involving nearly every factor which the records contain, is convincing that for these schools at least the records are highly dependable.

However, there is some tendency for even the best school records to understate the full situation regarding failure, while there is no corresponding tendency to overstate or to record failures not made. Not infrequently the pupils who drop out after previously failing may receive no mark or an incomplete one for the last semester in school. Although a portion or all of such work may obviously merit failure, yet it is not usually so recorded. In a similar manner pupils who remain in school one or two semesters or less, but take no examinations and receive no semester grades, might reasonably be considered to have failed if they shunned examinations merely to escape the recording of failures, as sometimes appears to be the case when judged from the incomplete grades recorded for only a part of the semester. A few pupils will elect to 'skip' the regular term examination, and then repeat the work of that semester, but no failures are recorded in such instances. Some teachers, when recording for their own subjects, prefer to indicate a failure by a dash mark or by a blank space until after the subject is satisfied later, and the passing mark is then filled in. One school indicates failure entirely by a short dash in the space provided, and then at times there occurs the 'cond' (conditioned) in pencil, apparently to avoid the classification as a failure by the usual sign. One finds some instances of a '?' or an 'inc' (incomplete) as a substitute for a mark of failure. Again, where there is no indication of failure recorded, the dates accompanying the grades for the subjects may tell the tale that two semesters were required to complete one semester's work in a subject. Some of these situations were easily discernible, and the indisputable failures treated as such in the succeeding tabulations; but in many instances this was not possible, and partial statement of these cases is all that is attempted.

How far these selected schools, their pupils, and the facts relating to them are representative or typical of the schools, the pupils, and the same facts for the states of New Jersey and New York, cannot be definitely known from the information that is now available. It seems indisputable, however, that the schools concerned in this study are at least among the better schools of these two states. If we may feel assured that the 6,141 pupils here included are fairly and generally representative of the facts for the eight schools to which they belong and which had an enrollment of 14,620 pupils in 1916; and if we are justified in classing these schools as averaging above the median rank of the schools for these states, then the statistical facts presented in the following pages may seem to be a rather moderate statement regarding the failures of high school pupils for the `states re-ferred to. It must be noted in this connection, however, that it is not unlikely that such schools, with their adequate records, will have the facts concerning failure more certainly recorded than will those whose records are incomplete, neglected, or poorly systematized.

A partial comparison of the teachers is possible between the schools represented here and those of New York and New Jersey. More than four hundred teachers comprised the teaching staff for the 6,141 pupils of the eight schools reported here. Of these about 40 per cent were men, while the percentage of men of all high school teachers in New Jersey and New York[4] was about 38 for the year 1916. The men in these schools comprised 50 per cent of the teachers in the subjects which prove most difficult by producing the most failures, and they were more frequently found teaching in the advanced years of these subjects. It is not assumed here that men are superior as high school teachers, but the endeavor is rather to show that the teaching force was by its constitution not unrepresentative. It may be added here that few high schools anywhere have a more highly selected and better paid staff of teachers than are found in this group of schools. It is indeed not easy to believe that the situation in these eight selected schools regarding failure and its contributing factors could not be readily duplicated elsewhere within the same states.

A SUMMARY OF CHAPTER I

The American people have a large faith in the public high school. It enrolls approximately 84 per cent of the secondary school pupils of the United States. High school attendance is becoming legally and vocationally compulsory. The size of the waste product demands a diagnosis of the facts. This study aims to discover the significant facts relative to the failing pupils.

Failure is used in the unit sense of non-passing in a semester subject. Failures are then counted in terms of these units.

This study includes 6,141 pupils belonging to eight different high schools and distributed throughout two states. The cumulative, official, school records for these pupils formed the basis of the data used.

The schools were selected primarily for their possession of adequate records. More dependable school records than those employed are not likely to be found, yet they tend to understate the facts of failure. It is quite possible that a superior school, and one with a high grade teaching staff, is actually selected by the requirements of the study.

REFERENCES:

1. *Annual Report of United States Commissioner of Education for 1917.*
2. Josslyn, H. W. Chapter IV, in Johnson's *Modern High School.*
3. *The Money Value of Education.* Bulletin No. 22, 1917, United States Bureau of Education.
4. New York and New Jersey *State School Reports for 1917.*

CHAPTER II

HOW EXTENSIVE ARE THE FAILURES OF THE HIGH SCHOOL PUPILS?

1. A DISTRIBUTION OF ALL ENTRANTS IN REFERENCE TO FAILURE

With no purpose of making this a comparative study of schools, the separate units or schools indicated in Chapter I will from this point be combined into a composite and treated as a single group. It becomes possible, with the complete and tabulated facts pertaining to a group of pupils, after their high school period has ended, to get a comprehensive survey of their school records and to answer such questions as: (1) What part of the total number of boys or of girls have school failures? (2) To what extent are the non-failing pupils the ones who succeed in graduating? (3) To what extent do the failing pupils withdraw early? The following tabulation will show how two of these questions are answered for the 6,141 pupils here reported on.

ALL ENTRANTS		FAILING	ALL GRADUATES	FAILING
Totals....	6,141	3,573 (58.2%)	1,936	1,125 (58.1%)
Boys......	2,646	1,645 (62.1%)	796	489 (61.4%)
Girls......	3,495	1,928 (55.1%)	1,140	639 (55.8%)

From this distribution we readily compute that the percentage of pupils who fail is 58.2 per cent (boys—62.1, girls—55.1). But this statement is itself inadequate. It does not take into account the 808 pupils who received no grades and had no chance to be classed as failing, but who were in most cases in school long enough to receive marks, and a portion of whom were either eliminated earlier or deterred from examinations by the expectation of failing. It seems entirely safe to estimate that no less than 60 per cent of this non-credited number should[1] be treated as of the failing group[2] of pupils. Then the percentage of pupils to be classed as failing in school subjects becomes 66 per cent (boys—69.6, girls—63.4).

12

In considering the second inquiry above, we find from the preceding distribution of pupils that 58.1 per cent (boys—61.4, girls—55.8) of all pupils that graduate have failed in one or more subjects one or more times. This percentage varies from 34 per cent to 73 per cent by schools, but in only two instances does the percentage fall below 50 per cent, and in one of these two it is almost 50 per cent.

We may now ask, when do the failing and the non-failing non-graduates drop out of school? Of the total number of non-graduates (4,205), there are 2,448 who drop out after failing one or more times, and 1,757 who drop out without failing. The cumulative percentages of the non-graduates in reference to dropping out are here given.

CUMULATIVE PERCENTAGES OF THE FAILING NON-GRADUATES
AS THEY ARE LOST BY SEMESTERS

LOST BY END OF SEMESTER	1	2	3	4	5	6	7	8	9
Per Cent	14.1	33.9	46.4	64.9	72.9	85.2	91.9	97.6	99.1

CUMULATIVE PERCENTAGES OF NON-FAILING NON-GRADUATES
AS THEY ARE LOST BY SEMESTERS

LOST BY END OF SEMESTER	1	2	3	4	5	6	7	8	9
Per Cent	61.1	78.0	85.9	92.1	94.5	98.4	99.5	....	....

Briefly stated, the above percentages assert that more than three fourths of those who neither fail nor graduate have left school by the end of the first year, while only 33.9 per cent of those non-graduates who fail have left so early. More than 50 per cent of the failing non-graduates continue in school to near the end of the second year. By that time about 90 per cent of the non-failing non-graduates have been lost from school. By a combination of the above groups we get the percentages of all non-graduates lost by successive semesters.

CUMULATIVE PERCENTAGES OF ALL NON-GRADUATES
LOST BY SUCCESSIVE SEMESTERS

LOST BY END OF SEMESTER	1	2	3	4	5	6	7	8
Per Cent	33.7	53.4	62.6	76.2	81.9	90.7	94.0	98.6

These percentages of non-graduates indicate that more than 50 per cent of those who do not graduate are gone by the end

of the first year, but that there are a few who continue beyond
four years without graduating.

2. The Later Distribution of Pupils by Semesters

Consideration is here given to the number of the total entrants
remaining in school for each successive semester, and then to
the accompanying percentages of failure for each group. The
following figures show the rapid decline in numbers.

The Persistence of Pupils in School, by Semesters

END OF SEMESTER	1	2	3	4	5	6	Graduate
6,141 (Total)........	4,723	3,893	3,508	2,935	2,697	2,234	1,936
Percentages.........	76.9	63.4	57.1	47.8	43.9	36.4	31.5

As was pointed out in Section 3 of Chapter I, the above
group does not include any increment to its own numbers by
means of transfer from other classes or schools. We find, accompanying this reduction in the number of pupils, which shows
more than 50 per cent gone by the end of the second year in
school, that there is no corresponding reduction in the percentage
of pupils failing each semester on the basis of the number of
those in school for that semester.

Percentage of Pupils Failing of the Pupils in School For That Period

Semesters.............	1	2	3	4	5	6	7	8
Per Cent..............	34.2	37.3	38.5	40.2	38.2	37.1	30.0	24.0

There is no difficulty in grasping the simple and definite significance of these figures, for they tell us that the percentage of
pupils failing increases for the first four semesters, slightly de-
clines for two semesters, with a greater decline for two more
semesters. These percentages of failures are based on the number of pupils enrolled at the beginning of the semester, and are
accordingly lower than the facts would really warrant since that
number is in each case considerably reduced by the end of the
same semester.

3. The Distribution of Failures

That the failures are widely distributed by semesters, by ages,
and for both boys and girls, is shown in Table I.

TABLE I

THE DISTRIBUTION OF FAILURES ACCORDING TO THE AGE AND THE SEMESTER OF THEIR OCCURRENCE*

SEMESTERS		12	13	14	15	16	17	18	19	20	21	22	UNDIS-TRIBUTED	TOTALS
1	B.	0	20	321	650	575	167	34	16	2	..	..	10	1795
	G.	1	19	356	813	611	236	67	3	0	..	..	13	2119
														3914
2	B.	..	2	95	423	534	256	57	27	4	..	..	5	1403
	G.	..	6	99	483	589	280	91	5	0	..	..	7	1560
														2963
3	B.	..	0	17	267	443	363	96	22	5	0	..	2	1215
	G.	..	1	28	318	548	317	99	15	0	2	..	1	1329
														2544
4	B.	..	..	5	101	437	403	169	32	7	2	..	5	1161
	G.	..	..	4	102	475	425	160	39	6	2	..	6	1219
														2380
5	B.	..	..	1	19	195	377	214	61	13	3	..	6	889
	G.	..	..	0	15	277	438	212	60	15	0	..	3	1020
														1909
6	B.	..	..	..	4	70	322	326	99	33	3	..	6	863
	G.	..	..	..	9	117	407	349	78	33	4	..	3	1000
														1863
7	B.	..	..	1	0	17	155	227	106	16	4	1	4	531
	G.	..	..	0	2	14	200	299	127	38	0	0	3	683
														1214
8	B.	..	..	..	..	0	42	173	109	49	2	..	5	380
	G.	..	..	..	..	2	58	244	140	49	10	..	3	506
														886
9	B.	..	..	..	..	..	0	31	32	18	1	..	..	82
	G.	..	..	..	..	..	4	39	67	31	5	..	..	146
														228
10	B.	..	..	..	..	..	..	1	16	9	3	0	..	29
	G.	..	..	..	..	..	..	3	13	10	3	1	..	30
														59
Sum-mary	B.	0	22	440	1464	2271	2085	1328	520	156	18	1	43	8348
	G.	1	26	487	1742	2633	2365	1563	547	182	26	1	39	9612
														17,960

* The expression of the above facts in terms of percentages for each age group was found to be difficult, since failures and not pupils are designated. But the total failures for each age group are expressed (on p. 36) as percentages of the entire number of subjects taken by these pupils for the semesters in which they failed. Such percentages increase as the ages rise. A similar statement of the percentages of failure by semesters will be found on p. 41.

Table I reads: the boys had 20 failures and the girls had 19 failures in the first semester and at the age of thirteen; in the second semester, at the age of thirteen, the boys had 2 failures and the girls 6. For each semester, the first line represents boys, the second line girls. There is a total of 17,960 failures listed in this table. In addition to this number there are 1,947 uncompleted grades for the failing non-graduates. The semes-

TABLE II

THE DISTRIBUTION OF FAILURES ACCORDING TO THE AGES AND THE SEMESTERS OF THEIR OCCURRENCE FOR THE GRADUATING PUPILS

SEMESTERS		13	14	15	16	AGES 17	18	19	20	21	22	TOTALS
1	B.	0	66	84	60	5	2	3	..	..	..	220
	G.	4	68	123	68	23	4	0	..	..	..	290
												510
2	B.	0	30	95	96	41	3	2	..	..	..	267
	G.	1	25	119	121	30	11	2	..	..	..	309
												576
3	B.	0	6	108	98	71	22	1	3	..	..	309
	G.	1	15	101	158	78	20	5	0	..	..	378
												687
4	B.	..	4	54	157	107	36	6	0	..	..	364
	G.	..	1	45	186	143	51	7	2	..	..	435
												799
5	B.	..	1	10	82	142	82	17	4	3	..	341
	G.	..	0	9	145	187	88	22	9	0	..	460
												801
6	B.	..	..	4	34	158	139	32	9	2	..	378
	G.	..	..	2	70	235	178	40	13	1	..	539
												917
7	B.	..	1	0	10	115	140	65	4	4	1	340
	G.	..	0	2	7	130	187	69	19	0	0	414
												754
8	B.	..	..	..	0	31	122	65	25	2	..	245
	G.	..	..	..	2	45	150	95	37	2	..	331
												576
9	B.	..	..	..	..	0	24	23	13	1	..	61
	G.	..	..	..	..	4	32	40	24	0	..	100
												161
10	B.	..	..	..	..	..	1	11	5	3	..	20
	G.	..	..	..	..	..	3	12	6	1	..	22
												42
Sum-mary	B.	..	108	355	537	670	571	225	63	15	1	2545
	G.	6	109	401	757	875	724	292	110	4	0	3278
												5823

In the facts which are involved and in the manner of reading them, this table is similar to Table I. The mode of the distribution of totals for the ages is at 17 in this table, Further reference will be made to both Tables I and II in later chapters of this study. (See pages 36, 37, 41, 42).

ters were frequently completed by such pupils but the records were left incomplete. Their previous records and their prospects of further partial or complete failure seem to justify an estimate of 55 per cent (1,070) of these uncompleted grades as either tentative or actual but unrecorded failures. Therefore we virtually have 1,070 other failures belonging to these pupils which are not included in Table I. Accordingly, since the number can only be estimated, the fact that they are not incorporated in that table suggests that the information which it discloses is something less than a full statement of the school failures for these pupils. In the distribution of the totals for ages, the mode appears plainly at 16, but with an evident skewness toward the upper ages. The failures for the years 16, 17, and 18, when added together, form 68.1 per cent of the total failures. If those for 15 years are also included, the result is 86 per cent of the total. Of the total failures, 65.7 per cent are found in the first two years (11,801 out of the total of 17,960). But the really striking fact is that 34.3 per cent of the failures occur after the end of the first two years, after 52.2 per cent of the pupils are gone, and with other hundreds leaving in each succeeding semester before even the end of the eighth. In Table II we have similar facts for the pupils who graduate.

A further analysis of the failures is here made in reference to the number of pupils and the number of failures each.

TABLE III

A DISTRIBUTION OF FAILING PUPILS ACCORDING TO THE NUMBER OF FAILURES PER PUPIL, IN EACH SEMESTER

No. of Failures		SEMESTERS 1	2	3	4	5	6	7	8	9	10	TOTALS
1	B.	459	430	375	352	271	221	157	113	22	11	2411
	G.	561	535	428	421	328	261	167	123	35	9	2868
								32.5%				5279
2	B.	271	242	211	206	149	144	79	68	19	4	1393
	G.	271	253	238	204	.177	142	127	84	17	6	1519
								34.9%				2912
3	B.	144	106	81	73	59	60	45	27	6	2	603
	G.	207	103	81	75	75	83	52	38	20	3	737
								35.%				1340
4	B.	83	39	33	30	27	32	10	10	1	1	266
	G.	95	50	38	35	27	39	19	19	3	0	325
								31.8%				591
5	B.	6	3	5	8	7	8	7	2	0	..	46
	G.	3	2	6	5	1	10	6	5	1	..	39
								55.3%				85
6	B.	...	...	3	3	0	1	1	...	...	..	8
	G.	...	...	...	...	...	...	...	...	..	..	..
								25.%				8
Tot.	B.	963	820	708	672	513	466	299	220	48	18	4727
	G.	1137	943	791	740	608	535	371	269	76	18	5488
												10,215

Table III tells us that 459 boys and 561 girls have one failure each in the first semester of their high school work; 271 boys and the same number of girls have two failures in the first semester, and so on, for the ten semesters and for as many as six failures per pupil. The failures represented by these pupils give a total of 17,960. A distribution of the total failures per pupil, and the facts relative thereto, will be considered in Chapter IV of this study.

The above distribution of Table III is repeated here in Table IV, so far as it relates to the failing graduates only.

TABLE IV

A DISTRIBUTION OF THE FAILING PUPILS WHO GRADUATE, ACCORDING TO THE NUMBER OF FAILURES PER PUPIL IN EACH SEMESTER

SEMESTERS

NO. OF FAILURES		1	2	3	4	5	6	7	8	9	10	TOTALS
1	B.	110	131	137	150	162	139	120	118	19	11	1097
	G.	136	142	181	200	197	180	121	89	20	3	1269
							50%					2366
2	B.	34	49	61	69	61	75	47	28	15	3	442
	G.	49	64	63	86	81	73	81	62	10	5	574
							53.2%					1016
3	B.	10	10	14	18	12	17	27	17	4	1	130
	G.	16	9	14	13	27	43	30	20	16	3	191
							67.6%					321
4	B.	3	2	2	3	4	8	6	5	0	..	33
	G.	2	3	6	6	5	16	9	12	3	..	62
							71.6%					95
5	B.	...	...	0	2	1	0	3	0	..	..	6
	G.	...	...	1	0	0	4	1	2	..	..	8
							78.6%					14
6	B.	...	...	...	...	...	1	1	..	..	..	2
	G.	...	...	...	...	0	0	...	..	..	..	0
							100%					2
Tot.	B.	157	192	214	237	240	240	204	163	48	15	1710
	G.	203	218	265	305	310	316	242	185	49	11	2104
												3814

This table reads similarly to Table III. There is not the element of continuous dropping out to be considered, as in Table III, until after the sixth semester is passed, for no pupils graduate in less than three years. The failures represented in this table number 5,823. This same distribution will be the subject of further comment later on. It discloses some facts that Table III tends to conceal, for instance, that the greater number of

graduating pupils who have 2, 3, 4, 5, and 6 failures in a semester
are found after the end of the second year.

4. DISTRIBUTION OF THE FAILURES IN REFERENCE TO THE SUB-
JECTS IN WHICH THEY OCCUR

The following tabulation of failures will show how they were
shared by both boys and girls in each of the school subjects
which provided the failures here listed.

NUMBER OF FAILURES DISTRIBUTED BY SCHOOL SUBJECTS

	Total	Math.	Eng.	Latin	Ger.	Fr.	Hist.	Sci.	Bus. Subj's.	Span. or Greek
B.	8348	2015	1555	1523	917	473	571	850	424	20
G.	9612	2300	1424	1833	812	588	1036	1013	593	13
Per Cent of Total		24.1	16.5	18.7	9.6	5.9	8.9	10.3	5.6	.2

The abbreviated headings above will be self-explanatory by
reference to section 3 of Chapter I. The first line of numbers
gives the failures for the boys, the second line for the girls.
Mathematics has 24.1 per cent of all the failures for all the
pupils. Latin claims 18.7 per cent and English 16.5 per cent of
all the failures. These three subjects make a total of nearly 60
per cent of the failures for the nine subject groups appearing
here. But still this is only a partial statement of the facts as
they are, since the total enrollment by subjects is an independent
matter and far from being equally divided among all the subjects
concerned. The subject enrollment may sometimes be relatively
high and the percentage of failure for that subject correspondingly lower than for a subject with the same number of failures
but a smaller enrollment. This fact becomes quite apparent
from the following percentages taken in comparison with the
ones just preceding:

PERCENTAGES ENROLLED IN EACH SUBJECT OF THE SUM TOTAL OF THE
SUBJECT ENROLLMENTS FOR ALL PUPILS AND ALL SEMESTERS

Math.	Eng.	Latin	Ger.	Fr.	Hist.	Sci.	Bus. Subj's.	Span. or Greek
17.3	24.0	11.9	8.5	6.8	10.2	12.5	8.3	.5

We note that the percentages for mathematics and English,
which represent their portions of the grand total of subject enrollments, are virtually the reverse of the percentages which

designate the amount of total failures produced by the same two subjects. That means that the percentage of the total failures produced by mathematics is really greater than was at first apparent, while the percentages of failures for English is not so great relatively as the statement of the total failures above would alone indicate. In a similar manner, we note that Latin has 18.7 per cent of all the failures, but its portion of the total enrollment for all subjects is only 11.9 per cent. If the failures in this subject were in proportion to the enrollment, its percentage of the failures would be reduced by 6.8 per cent. On the other hand, if the failures for English were in the same proportion to the total as is its subject enrollment, it would claim 7.5 per cent more of all the failures. In the same sense, French, history, science, and the business subjects have a smaller proportion of all the failures than of all the subject enrollments.

The comparison of failures by subjects may be continued still further by computing the percentage of failures in each subject as based on the number enrolled in that subject. Such percentages are here presented for each subject.

PERCENTAGE OF THE NUMBER TAKING THE SUBJECT WHO FAIL
IN THAT SUBJECT

Latin	Math.	Ger.	Fr.	Hist.	Sci.	Eng.	Bus. Subj's.	Span. or Greek
18.7	16.0	13.5	11.6	10.4	9.8	8.2	8.0	4.1

It becomes evident at once that the largest percentage of failures, based on the pupils taking the subject, is in Latin, although we have already found that mathematics has the greatest percentage of all the failures recorded (p. 19). But here mathematics follows Latin, with German coming next in order as ranked by its high percentage of failure for those enrolled in the subject. History has the median percentage for the failures as listed for the nine subjects above.

The failures as reported by subjects for other schools and other pupils will provide a comparison which may indicate something of the relative standing of this group of schools in reference to failures. The failures are presented below for thirteen high schools in New Jersey, involving 24,895 grades, as reported by D. C. Bliss[3] in 1917. As the schools were reported singly, the

median percentage of failure for each subject is used here for
our purpose. But Mr. Bliss' figures are computed from the promotion sheets for June, 1915, and include none of those who had
dropped out. In this sense they are not comparable to the percentages of failure as presented in this study. Yet with the one
exception of Latin these median percentages are higher. The
percentages as presented below for St. Paul[4] are in each case
based on the total number taking the subject for a single semester, and include about 4,000 pupils, in all the classes, in the
four high schools of the city.*

The facts presented for St. Louis[5] are for one school only,
with 2,089 pupils, as recorded for the first half of the year
1915-16. All foreign languages as reported for this school are
grouped together. History is the only subject that has a percentage of failure lower than that of the corresponding subjects
for our eight schools. The figures for both St. Paul and St.
Louis are based on the grades for all classes in school, but for
only a single semester. One cannot avoid feeling that a statement of facts for so limited a period may or may not be dependable and representative for all periods. The percentages for
Paterson[6] are reported for about 4,000 pupils, in all classes, for
two successive semesters, and are based on the number examined. For Denver,[7] the records are reported for 4,120 pupils,
and cover a two-year period. The percentages for Butte[8] are
based on the records for 3,110 pupils, for one school semester.
The figures reported by Rounds and Kingsbury[9] are for only

PERCENTAGES OF FAILURE BY SUBJECTS—QUOTED FOR OTHER SCHOOLS

	Math.	Latin	Ger.	Fren.	Eng.	Hist	Sci.	Bus. Subj's.
13 N. J. H. S's.	20.0	18.0	16.0	..	14.0	11.0	..	11.5
St. Paul.......	21.8	13.6	14.3	17.0	10.0	10.9	7.3	11.7
St. Louis......	18.0	[——16——]			13.0	7.0	19.0	..
Paterson.......	23.1	21.6	23.4	..	12.2	13.9	18.3	8.5
Denver........	24.0	21.0	12.0	..	11.7	11.0	17.0	11.0
Butte..........	18.6	25.0	24.0	32.6	5.4	7.0	13.0	8.4
R and K......	24.7	.	..	..	18.5	..	..	..
Our 8 H. S's...	16.0	18.7	13.5	11.6	8.2	10.4	9.8	8.0

* It is a significant fact, and one worthy of note here, that the report for St. Paul is
apparently the only one of the surveys which also states the number taking each subject,
as well as the percentages of failure. Percentages alone do not tell the whole story, and
they do not promote the further utilization of the facts to discover other relationships.

two subjects, but for forty-six widely separated high schools, whose enrollment for these two subjects was 57,680.

In some schools the reports were not available for all subjects. It is not at all probable, so far as information could be obtained, that the failures of the drop-out pupils for any of the schools were included in the percentages as reported above, or that the percentages are based on the total number in the given subjects, with the exception of one school. Moreover, it is certain for at least some of the schools that neither the failures of the drop-outs nor the pupils who were in the class for less than a whole semester were considered in the percentages above. So far, however, as these comparisons may be justified, the suggestion made in Chapter I that the schools included in this study are doubtless a superior group with respect to failures appears to be strengthened by the comparisons made above.

It becomes more apparent, as we attempt to offer a statement of failures as taken from the various reports, that they are not truly comparable. The bases of such percentages are not at all uniform. The basis used most frequently is the number enrolled at the end of the period rather than the total number enrolled for any class, for which the school has had to provide, and which should most reasonably form the basis of the percentage of failure. Furthermore, the failures for pupils who drop out are not usually counted. Yet, in most of the reports, the situation is not clearly indicated for either of the facts referred to. Still more difficult is the task of securing a general statement of failures by subjects, since the percentages are most frequently reported separately for each class, in each subject, and for different buildings, but with the number of pupils stated for neither the failures nor the enrollment. The St. Paul report[4] is an exception in this regard.

To present the full situation it is indeed necessary to know the failures for particular teachers, subjects, and buildings, but it is also frequently necessary to be able to make a comparison of results for different systems. Consequently, in order to use the varied reports for the attempted comparison above, the plan was pursued of averaging the percentages as stated for the different classes, semesters, and years of a subject, in each school separately, and then selecting the median school thus determined as the one best representing the city or the system. This method was employed to modify the reports, and to secure the percentages as stated above for Denver, Patterson, and Butte. Any plan of averaging the percentages for the four years of English, or similarly for any other subject, may actually tend to misstate the facts, when the percentages or the numbers represented are not very nearly equal. But, in an incidental way, the difficulty serves to emphasize the inadequacy and the incomparability in the reporting of failures as found in the various studies, as well as to warn us of the hopelessness of reaching any conclusions apart from a knowledge of the procedure employed in securing the data.

The basis is also provided for some interesting comparisons by isolating from the general distribution of failures by school subjects (p. 19) the same facts for the failing graduates. That gives the following distribution.

THE FAILURES BY SCHOOL SUBJECTS FOR GRADUATES ONLY

Total	Math.	Eng.	Latin	Ger.	Fr.	Hist.	Sci.	Bus. Subj's.	Span. or Greek
5803 B.	660	403	521	241	191	180	251	91	7
6334 G.	782	347	673	257	240	410	394	162	12
Per Cent of Totals	24.8	12.9	20.5	8.5	7.4	10.1	11.	4.3	.3

SIMILAR PERCENTAGES FOR THE NON-GRADUATES

As above	23.6	18.3	17.7	10.1	5.3	8.4	10.	6.3	.1

It is a noteworthy fact that the percentages of failure (based on the total failures for the graduates) run higher in mathematics, Latin, history, French, and science for the graduates than for the whole composite number (page 19). The non-graduates have a correspondingly lower percentage of failure in these subjects, as is indicated above. The school influences in respect to the failures of the non-graduates differ from those of the graduates chiefly in the fact that the failures of the former tend to occur to a greater extent in the earlier years of these subjects, since so many of the non-graduates are in the school for only those earlier years; while the failures of the graduates range more widely and have a tendency to predominate in the upper years of the subject, as will be further emphasized in the later pages of this report (see also Table IV).

5. Distribution of Pupils Dropping Out—Semesters—Ages

Table V presents the facts concerning the time and the age at which the failing pupils drop out of school. Table VI furnishes the corresponding facts for the non-failing drop-outs.

TABLE V

Distribution of the Failing Non-Graduates, Showing the Semester and the Age at the Time of Dropping Out

SEMESTERS		13	14	15	16	AGES 17	18	19	20	21	22	UNDISTRIB.	TOTALS
1	B.	1	40	49	50	18	0	1	1	..	..	1	160
	G.	3	40	65	47	23	4	0	0	..	..	3	185
													345
2	B.	..	9	56	88	56	22	6	2	..	..	3	242
	G.	..	6	72	119	61	24	3	0	..	..	6	291
													533
3	B.	..	4	30	40	23	10	7	..	..	..	0	114
	G.	..	3	35	51	32	13	7	..	..	..	1	142
													256
4	B.	..	1	16	66	86	34	16	2	..	..	3	224
	G.	..	1	19	60	70	59	18	3	..	..	0	230
													454
5	B.	..	..	2	12	36	21	8	4	..	..	3	86
	G.	..	..	4	17	48	28	9	3	..	..	1	110
													196
6	B.	..	..	1	6	48	52	38	10	..	..	1	156
	G.	..	..	1	11	52	49	26	5	..	..	2	146
													302
7	B.	..	..	..	2	12	35	21	7	0	..	1	78
	G.	..	..	..	2	15	21	15	4	1	..	0	59
													137
8	B.	..	..	..	0	10	23	19	19	2	0	2	75
	G.	..	..	..	2	10	31	29	10	4	2	3	91
													166
9	B.	..	..	..	..	1	4	4	2	..	1	1	13
	G.	..	..	..	..	1	6	12	4	..	0	0	23
													36
10	B.	..	..	..	..	..	..	1	3	3	1	..	8
	G.	..	..	..	..	..	..	4	3	3	1	..	11
													19
11	B.	..	..	..	..	..	..	..	0	0	0	..	0
	G.	..	..	..	..	..	..	..	2	1	1	..	4
													4
Tot.	B.	1	54	154	264	290	201	120	50	6	2	14	1156
	G.	3	50	196	309	312	235	123	34	9	4	16	1292
													2448

Table V reads: In the first semester 1 boy and 3 girls drop out at age 13; 40 boys and 40 girls drop out at the age of 14; 49 boys and 65 girls, at the age of 15. In this table, as elsewhere, age 15 means from 14½ to 15½, and so on. Any drop-out, as for the second semester, means either during or at the end of that semester.

TABLE VI

DISTRIBUTION OF THE NON-FAILING NON-GRADUATES, SHOWING THE SEMESTER AND THE AGE AT THE TIME OF DROPPING OUT

SEMESTERS		13	14	15	16	17	18	19	20	21	TOTALS	
1	B.	17	118	141	106	39	3	4	1	1	430	
	G.	11	159	235	160	51	19	4	4	0	643	
												1073
2	B.	0	7	49	50	18	7	3	0	..	134	
	G.	1	1	59	42	31	10	7	2	..	163	
												297
3	B.	..	..	7	16	11	5	1	0	..	40	
	G.	..	..	14	22	33	15	3	2	..	89	
												129
4	B.	..	..	5	13	11	10	1	0	1	41	
	G.	..	..	7	20	31	16	2	1	1	78	
												119
5	B.	..	..	1	2	9	1	2	0	..	15	
	G.	..	..	0	3	10	9	4	1	..	27	42
6	B.	..	..	1	4	14	3	2	0	..	24	
	G.	..	..	0	5	17	13	7	3	..	45	
												69
7	B.	..	..	..	0	2	2	2	1	..	7	
	G.	..	..	..	1	2	7	1	1	..	12	
												19
8	B.	..	..	..	..	..	1	1	1	..	3	
	G.	..	..	..	..	..	3	1	1	..	5	
												8
9	B.	..	..	..	..	..	..	..	0	..	0	
	G.	..	..	..	..	..	..	..	1	..	1	
												1
Tot.	B.	17	125	204	191	104	32	16	3	2	694	
	G.	12	170	315	253	175	92	29	16	1	1063	
												1757

Table VI reads similarly to Table V. The distribution of the age totals for the pupils dropping out gives us medians which, for both boys and girls, fall within the 17-year group for the failing pupils, but within the 16-year group for the non-failing pupils. For Table V the mode of the distribution is at 17, but for Table VI it is at 15. The percentages of dropping out for each age group are given below. First, all the pupils of Tables V and VI are grouped together for this purpose, then the boys and the girls for Tables V and VI are considered separately to facilitate the comparison of facts.

PERCENTAGES IN EACH AGE GROUP OF THE TOTAL NUMBER DROPPING OUT

Ages	13	14	15	16	17	18	19	20	21
Per Cent	0.8	9.5	20.7	24.2	21.0	13.3	6.8	2.4	1.2

It is readily seen from the above percentages that, as would be expected, the drop-outs are most frequent for the very ages which are most common in the high school. There is no special accumulation of drop-outs for either the earlier or the later ages. But, if in any semester we consider the drop-outs for each age as a percentage of the total pupils represented for that age, the facts are more fully revealed, as is indicated below for certain semesters.

PERCENTAGES OF DROP-OUTS FOR EACH AGE, ON THE TOTALS FOR SUCH AGE IN THE FIRST, SECOND AND FOURTH SEMESTERS

AGES

	13	14	15	16	17	18	19	20	21
Semester 1	6.8	18.2	23.1	32.6	38.3	35.0	40.0	40.0	..
Semester 2	4.0	8.1	14.8	18.3	22.2	30.0	40.0	33.0	..
Semester 4	0	9.0	11.8	12.5	16.5	24.6	35.2	50.0	..

If these semesters may be taken as indicative of all, an almost steady increase will be expected in the percentages of drop-outs as the ages of the pupils rise. It follows, then, that the older ages have the higher percentages of drop-outs when this basis of the computation is employed. We may, however, make some helpful comparisons of the ages of drop-outs for boys and for girls by merely using the percentages of total drop-outs for the purpose.

PERCENTAGES OF FAILING DROP-OUTS IN EACH AGE GROUP, FOR BOYS AND GIRLS SEPARATELY

AGES

	13	14	15	16	17	18	19	20	21
Boys	0	4.6	12.5	22.8	25.1	17.4	10.3	4.3	1.9
Girls	.2	3.8	15.1	23.9	24.1	19.0	9.5	2.6	2.2

Here it appears that, of all the boys and girls who fail before dropping out, the school loses at the age of 14, for example, 4.6 per cent for the boys and 3.8 per cent for the girls. As a matter of mere convenience, the percentages for age 21 are made to include also the undistributed pupils in Table V.

PERCENTAGES OF THE NON-FAILING DROP-OUTS IN EACH AGE GROUP, FOR
BOYS AND GIRLS SEPARATELY

AGES

	13	14	15	16	17	18	19	20
Boys	2.4	18.0	29.4	27.1	15.0	4.4	2.3	0.7
Girls	1.1	16.0	29.6	23.8	16.4	8.6	2.7	1.6

These percentages are computed from the age totals in Table
VI, just as the ones preceding are computed from Table V. It
seems worthy of note here that close to 50 per cent of the non-
failing drop-outs occur under 16 years of age, for both the boys
and the girls; but that the number of the failing pupils who drop
out does not reach 20 per cent for the boys or the girls in these
same years. It is likewise remarkable in these distributions that
the percentages for boys and for girls show such slight differences in either of the two groupings.

SUMMARY OF CHAPTER II

If to the recorded failures the virtual but unrecorded ones
are added, the percentage of failing pupils is 66 per cent.
This percentage is higher for the boys than for the girls by a
difference of 6 per cent.

Of the graduating pupils, 58.1 per cent fail one or more times.

Of the non-failing non-graduates 78 per cent are lost from
school by the end of their first year. But the failing non-graduates have not lost such a percentage before the end of the third
year.

The percentage of pupils failing increases for the first four
semesters, and lowers but little for two more semesters. One
third to one half of the pupils fail in each semester to seventh.

In the distribution of failures by ages and semesters, 86 per
cent are found from ages 15 to 18 inclusive. Thirty-four per
cent of the failures occur after the end of the second year, when
52.2 per cent of the pupils have been lost and others are leaving
continuously.

Mathematics, Latin, and English head the list in the percentages of total failures, and together provide nearly 60 per cent of
the failures; but English has a large subject-enrollment to balance its count in failures.

Mathematics, Latin, and German fail the highest percentages on the number of pupils taking the subjects.

In several subjects the percentages of failure based. on the total failures are higher for the graduates than for the non-graduates.

For the pupils dropping out without failure the median age is at 16, with the mode at 15. For the failing drop-outs both the median and the mode are at the age of 17. Nearly 50 per cent of the non-failing drop-outs occur under age 16, but not 20 per cent of the failing non-graduates are gone by that age. The percentage of drop-outs is higher for older pupils.

REFERENCES

1. Kelley, T. L. "A Study of High School and University Grades, with Reference to Their Intercorrelation and the Causes of Elimination," *Journal of Educational Psychology*, 6:365.
2. Johnson, G. R. "Qualitative Elimination in High School," *School Review*, 18:680.
3. Bliss, D. C. "High School Failures," *Educational Administration and Supervision*, Vol. 3.
4. Strayer, G. D., Coffman, L. D., Prosser, C. A. *Report of a Survey of the School System of St. Paul, Minnesota.*
5. Meredith, A. B. *Survey of the St. Louis Public Schools*, 1917, Vol. III, p. 51.
6. *Annual Report of the Board of Education, Paterson, New Jersey*, 1915.
7. Bobbitt, J. F. *Report of the School Survey of Denver*, 1916.
8. Strayer, G. D. *A Survey of the Public Schools of Butte*, 1914.
9. Rounds, C. R., Kingsbury, H. B. "Do Too Many Students Fail?" *School Review*, 21:585.

CHAPTER III

WHAT BASIS IS DISCOVERABLE FOR PROGNOSTI-CATING THE OCCURRENCE OF OR THE NUMBER OF FAILURES?

1. ATTENDANCE, MENTAL OR PHYSICAL DEFECTS, AND SIZE OF CLASSES ARE POSSIBLE FACTORS

Any definite factors available for the school that have a prognostic value in reference to school failures will help to perform a function quite comparable to the science of preventive medicine in its field, and in contrast with the older art of doctoring the malady after it has been permitted to develop. Such prognostication of failure, however, need not imply a complete knowledge of the causes of the failures. It may simply signify that in certain situations the causes are less active or are partly overcome by other factors.

Perhaps one of the simplest factors with a prognostic value on failure may be found in the facts of attendance. Persistent or repeated absence from school may reach a point where it tends to affect the number of failures. It happened, unfortunately, that the reports for attendance were incomplete or lacking in a considerable portion of the records employed in this study. Consequently the influence of attendance is given no especial consideration in these pages, except as explained in Chapter I, that the pupil must have been present enough of any semester to secure his subject grades, else no failure is counted and no time is charged to his period in school. In this connection, Dr. C. H. Keyes[1] found in a study of elementary school pupils that of 1,649 pupils losing four weeks or more in a single year 459 belonged to the accelerate pupils, 647 to those arrested, and 543 to pupils normal in their school work. He accredits such large loss of time as almost invariably the result of illness and of contagious disease. He also says, "Prolonged absence from school is appreciable in producing arrest especially when it amounts to more than 25 days in one school year." But the diseases of childhood, with the resultant absence, are less prevalent in the high school years than earlier. Furthermore, the losses due to change of residence will not be met with here, for, as explained in Chapter I, no transferred pupils are included subsequent to the time of the transference either to or from the school.

The influence of physical or mental defects also deserves recognition here as a possible factor relative to school failures, although this study has no data to offer of any statistical value in that regard. A few pupils in high school may actually reach the limits prescribed by their ' intelligence quotient '[2] or general mental ability, or perhaps, as Bronner[3] so interestingly points out, be handicapped by some special mental disability. If such be true, they will doubtless be found in the number of school drop-outs later referred to as failing in 50 per cent or more of their work; but we have no measurement of intelligence recorded for them to serve our purposes of prognostication. In the matter of physical defects alone, the report of Dr. L. P. Ayres[4] on a study of 3,304 pupils, ten to fourteen years old, in New York City, states that "In every case except in that of vision the children rated as ' dull ' are found to be suffering from physical defects to a greater degree than ' normal ' or ' bright ' children." The defects of vision, which is the exception noted, may be even partly the result of the studious habits of the pupils. Bronner[3] remarks on the " relationships between mental and physical conditions," and also on how " the findings on tests were altogether different after the child had been built up physically." But Gulick and Ayres[5] conclude that it is evident from the facts at hand that if vision were omitted the percentage of defects would dwindle and become comparatively small among the upper grades. This would probably be still more true for the high school; but this whole field has not yet been completely and thoroughly investigated.

It would be very desirable to have ascertained the size of the classes in which the failures were most frequent, as well as the relative success of the pupils repeating subjects in larger or in smaller classes. But, as such facts were unobtainable, it is permitted here simply to recognize the possible influence of this factor. It seems deserving in itself of careful and special study. From the standpoint of the pupil, the kind of subject, the kind of teacher, and the sort of discipline employed will tend to influence the size of class to be called normal, and to make it a sort of variable. Thirty pupils is regarded by the North Central Association as the maximum size of class in high school.[6] Surely the size of class will react on the pupil by affecting the teacher's spirit and energy. Reference is made by Hall-Quest[7] to an experiment, whose author is not named, in which 829 pupils stated that their " most helpful teachers were pleasant, cheerful, optimistic, enthusiastic, and young." If such be true then the very large size of classes will tend to reduce the teacher's helpfulness.

2. The Employment of the School Entering Age for Prognosis

A promising but less emphasized basis of prognosticating the school success or failure of the pupils is found in the employment of the school entering ages for this purpose. The distribution of all the pupils (except 30 undistributed ones, for whom the records were incomplete), according to entering age, is here presented, independently for the boys and for the girls.

DISTRIBUTION OF PUPILS BY THEIR ENTRANCE AGES TO HIGH SCHOOL

AGES

Total	12	13	14	15	16	17	18	19	20	Undistributed
2646 B.	16	211	820	900	497	148	23	10	7	14
3495 G.	8	259	1124	1217	614	194	51	10	8	16

The entering ages of these 6,141 pupils are distributed from 12 to 20, with 30 of them for whom the age records were not given. The median age for all the entrants is 15.3. But in order to compare this with the median entering age (14.9) of the 1,033 pupils reported by King[8] for the Iowa City high school, or with the median entering age (14.5) of 1000 high school pupils in New York City, as reported by Van Denburg,[9] it is necessary to reduce these medians to the same basis of age classification. Since age 15 for this study starts at 14½, then 15.3 would be only 14.8 (15.3 — .5) as by their classification. The percentages of the total number of pupils for each age are given below.

PERCENTAGES OF PUPILS FOR EACH ENTERING AGE

AGES

	12	13	14	15	16	17	18	19	20
								Undistributed	
Total......	0.4	7.6	31.6	34.4	18.1	5.5	1.2	1.0	
Boys	0.6	8.0	31.0	37.8	18.8	5.6	0.8	1.1	
Girls......	0.2	7.4	32.4	34.8	17.5	5.5	1.4	1.0	

We see that 84 per cent of the pupils enter at age 14, 15, and 16, or, what is perhaps more important, that nearly 40 per cent enter under 15 years of age. The similarity of percentages for boys and for girls is pronounced. The slight advantage of the boys for ages 12 and 13 may be due to home influence in restricting the early entrance of the girls, thus causing a corresponding superiority for the girls at age 14. The mode of this percentage distribution is at 15 for both boys and girls.

What portion of each entering-age-group has no failures? This question and the answer presented below direct our attention to the superiority of the pupils of the earlier entering ages. That these groups of earlier ages of entrance are comprised of pupils selected for their capabilities is shown by the successive decrease in the percentages of the non-failing as the ages of their entrance increases, up to age 18.

DISTRIBUTION OF THE PUPILS WHO DO NOT FAIL, FOR EACH
ENTERING-AGE-GROUP

AGES

	12	13	14	15	16	17	18	19	20
Totals									
1001 B	11	102	320	309	186	56	9	4	4
1574 G.........	3	133	522	545	256	73	29	7	6
% of Entrants.	58.0	50.0	43.4	40.0	39.8	37.7	55.0		

Here is definite evidence that the pupils of the earlier entering ages are less likely to fail in any of their school subjects than are the older ones. Those entering at ages 12 or 13 escape school failures altogether for 50 per cent or more of their numbers. Those entering at age 14 are somewhat less successful but still seem superior to those of later entrance ages. It is encouraging, then, that these three ages of entrance include nearly 40 per cent of the 6,141 pupils. There is, of course, nothing in this situation to justify any deduction of the sort that pupils entering at the age of 17 would have been more successful had they been sent to high school earlier, except that had they been able to enter high school earlier they would have represented a different selection of ability by that fact alone. There is also a sort of selection operative for the pupils entering at ages 18, 19, or 20, which tends to account at least partly for the rise in the percentage of the non-failing for these years. It is safe to believe that for the most part only the more able, ambitious, and purposeful individuals are likely to display the energy required or to discern the need of their entering high school when they have reached the age of 18 or later. The appeal of school athletics will in this case seem very inadequate to explain their entrance so late, since the girls predominate so strongly for these years. Then it may be contended further that the added maturity and experience of those later entrants may partly compensate for a lack of native ability, if such be the case, and thereby result in a relatively high percentage of non-failing pupils for this group.

It is readily conceded that the avoidance of failure in school work serves as only one criterion for gauging the pupils' accomplishment. It is accordingly important to inquire how the different age-groups of school entrants compare with reference to the persistence and ability which is represented by school graduation. A truly striking array of percentages follows in reference to the question of how many of the entering pupils in each age-group do graduate.

DISTRIBUTION OF THE PUPILS GRADUATING FOR EACH ENTERING-AGE GROUP

AGES									
Totals	12	13	14	15	16	17	18	19	20
796 B........	14	115	290	253	99	20	2	1	2
1140G........	5	151	465	363	124	26	5	1	0
% of Entrants.	79.1	56.6	38.8	29.9	20.0	13.4	9.4	10.0	13.3

These percentages bear convincing testimony in support of the previous evidence that the pupils of the earlier entering years are highly selected in ability.   Of all the high school entrants they are the 'most fit,' the least likely to fail, and the most certain to graduate.   The percentage of pupils graduating who entered at the age of 12 is approximately four times that of pupils who entered at the age of 16.   Thirteen is more than four times as fruitful of graduates as age 17; fourteen bears a similar relationship to age 18; and the percentage for fifteen is three times that for age 19, as is apparent from the above figures. The fact that the decline of these percentages ceases at age 19 is probably due to the greater maturity of such later entrants.

When we make inquiry as to what portion of the graduates in each of the above groups 'goes through' in four years or less, we get the series of percentages indicated below.

PERCENTAGE OF THE GRADUATES WHO FINISH IN FOUR YEARS OR LESS, FOR EACH OF THE ENTERING-AGE GROUPS

Ages	12	13	14	15	16	17	18
% of Each Group	84.2	85.7	75.8	79.5	84.3	80.4	100

It appears that the ones in the older age-groups who do graduate are not so handicapped in reference to the time requirement for graduation as we might have expected them to be from the facts of the preceding pages.   Perhaps that fact is partly accounted for by the not unusual tendency to restrain the more rapid progress of the younger pupils or to promote the older ones partly by age, so that by our school procedure the younger and the brighter pupils may at times actually be more retarded, according to mental age, than are the older and slower ones.

Since the same teachers, the same schools, and the same administrative policy were involved for the different entrance-age groups, the prognostic value of the factor of age at entrance will seem to be unimpaired, whether it operates independently as a gauge of rank in mental ability, or conjointly with and indicative of the varying influence on these pupils of other concomitant factors, such as the difference of economic demands, the difference of social interests, the difference in permanence of conflicting habits of the individual, or the difference in effectiveness of the school's appeal as adapted for the several ages.   One may contend, and with some success, that the high school régime is better adjusted to the younger pupils, with the consequent result that they are more successful in its requirements. The distractions of more numerous social interests may actually accompany the later years of school age. In reference to the social distractions of girls, Margaret Slattery says,[10] " This mania for ' going ' seizes many of our girls just when they need rest and natural pleasures, the great out-of-doors, and early hours of retiring." But surely such distractions are not peculiar to the girls alone. The economic needs that arise at the age of sixteen and later are often considered to constitute a pressing factor regarding the continuance in school. But VanDenburg[9] was convinced by the investigation, in New York City, of 420 rentals for the families of pupils that " on the whole the economic status of these pupils seems to be only a slight factor in their continuance in school." A similar conclusion was reached by Wooley,[11] in Cincinnati, after investigating 600 families, in which it was estimated that 73 per cent of the families did not need the earnings of the children who left school to go to work. The corresponding report by a commission[12] in Massachusetts shows 76 per cent. The same facts for New York City[13] indicate that 80 per cent of such families are independent of the child's wages. But Holley concludes,[14] from a study of certain towns in Illinois, that " there is a high correlation between the economic, educational, and social advantages of a home and the number of years of school which its children receive." It will hardly be denied that even aside from the relation of the family means to the school persistence, the economic needs may have a direct influence on the failing of the children in their school work, either because home conditions may be decidedly unfavorable for required home study, or because of the larger portion of time that must be given to outside employment, with its consequent reduction of the normal vitality of the individual or of his readiness to study. But, in spite of the possible interrelationship of these factors, it still appears that the school entrance age of pupils will serve as a valuable sort of educational compass to foretell in part the probable direction of their later accomplishment.

3. The Amount of Failure at Each Age and Its Relation to the Possibility of Failing for That Age

We have considered at some length the prognostic value of the age at entrance. Here we shall briefly consider the prognostic value of age in reference to the time when failures occur and the amount of failure for such age. If we were to total all the failures for a given age, as shown in Table I, what part will that form of the total subjects taken by these pupils at the time the failures occur? In other words, what are the percentages formed by the total failures on the possibility of failing, for the same pupils and the same semesters, considered by age groups? The summary line of Table I gives the total failures according to the ages at which they occurred. The number of pupils sharing in each group of these failures is also known by a separate tabulation. Then the full number of subjects per pupil is taken as 4½, since approximately 50 per cent of the pupils take five or more subjects each semester and the other 50 per cent take four or less (see p. 61). With the number of pupils given, and with a schedule of 4½ subjects per pupil, we are able to compute the percentages which the failures form of the total subjects for these failing pupils at the time. These percentages are given below.

The Percentages Formed by Failures at Each Age on the Possibilities of Failing at That Age and Time, for the Same Pupils

Ages	13	14	15	16	17	18	19	20	21
%	36.6	38.0	37.9	40.9	40.8	41.2	41.3	42.0	42.7

These percentages are computed from the data secured in Table I, as noted above.

There is an almost unbroken rise in these percentages from 36.6 for age 13 to 42.7 for age 21. Not only do a greater number of the older pupils fail, as was previously indicated, but they also have a greater percentage of failure for the subjects which they are taking. It seems appropriate here to offer a caution that, in reading the above percentages, one must not conclude that all of age 14 fail in 38 per cent of their work, but rather that those who do fail at age 14 fail in 38 per cent of their work for that semester. The evidence does not seem to indicate that the maturity of later years operates to secure any general reduction of these percentages. The prognostic value of such facts seems to consist in leading us to expect a greater percentage of failures (on the total subjects) from the older pupils who fail than from the younger ones who fail. If it were possible to translate the above percentages to a basis of the possibility of failure for all pupils, instead of the possibility for failing pupils only, the disparity for the different ages would become more pronounced, as the earlier ages have more nonfailing pupils. But this we are not able to do, as our data are not adequate for that purpose.

4. The Initial Record in High School for Prognosis of Failure

For this purpose the pupil record for the first year, in reference to failures, is deemed more adequate and dependable than the record for the first semester only. Accordingly, the pupils have been classified on their first year's record into those who had 0, 1, 2, 3, and up to 7 or more failures. Then these groups were further distributed into those who failed 0, 1, 2, 3, and up to 7 or more times after the first year. From such a double distribution we may get some indication of what assurance the first year's record offers on the expectation of later failures. Table VII presents these facts.

Table VII is read in this manner: Of all the pupils who have 0 failures the first year (805 boys, and 1,129 girls) 397 boys and 672 girls have 0 failures later, 105 boys and 130 girls have 1 failure later, 77 boys and 98 girls have 2 failures later, while 68 boys and 63 girls have seven or more failures later. The column of totals to the right gives the pupils for each number of failures for the first year. The line of totals at the bottom gives the pupils for each number of failures subsequent to the first year.

The table includes 3,508 pupils, since those who did not remain in school more than three semesters are not included (1,120 boys, 1,513 girls). Obviously, those who do not stay more than one year would have no subsequent school record, and those remaining only a brief time beyond one year would not have a record of comparable length. It seems quite significant, too, for the purposes of our prognosis, that of the 2,633 pupils dropping out in three semesters or less only about 43 per cent have ever failed (boys—46 per cent, girls—41 per cent).. In contrast to this, nearly 70 per cent (69.6) of those continuing in school more than three semesters fail one or more times. Those who drop out without failure, in the three semesters or less, constitute nearly 60 per cent of the total non-failing pupils (2,568), but the failing pupils who drop out in that same period constitute less than 32 per cent of the total who fail (3,573). This situation received some emphasis in Chapter II and will be further treated in Chapter IV, under the comparison of the failing and non-failing groups.

TABLE VII

SUBSEQUENT RECORD OF FAILURES FOR PUPILS FAILING 1, 2, 3, ETC., TIMES THE FIRST YEAR

FAILURES OF 1ST YEAR		FAILURES SUBSEQUENT TO FIRST YEAR								
		0	1	2	3	4	5	6	7+	TOTALS
0	B	397	105	77	50	47	37	24	68	805
	G	672	130	98	60	53	27	26	63	1129
		1069	235	175	110	100	64	50	131	1934
1	B	46	43	34	33	35	21	15	46	273
	G	65	43	53	33	33	19	17	67	330
		111	86	87	66	68	40	32	113	603
2	B	22	24	23	23	30	21	13	57	213
	G	42	32	27	21	22	13	15	83	255
		64	56	50	44	52	34	28	140	468
3	B	7	5	16	10	10	13	10	30	101
	G	8	9	7	10	17	6	7	41	105
		15	14	23	20	27	19	17	71	206
4	B	6	8	5	7	7	11	7	23	74
	G	8	7	5	6	10	8	4	27	75
		14	15	10	13	17	19	11	50	149
5	B	3	1	0	2	1	5	3	11	26
	G	5	9	5	6	5	4	2	14	50
		8	10	5	8	6	9	5	25	76
6	B	0	1	4	2	1	1	1	10	20
	G	2	1	2	2	6	2	0	6	21
		2	2	6	4	7	3	1	16	41
7+	B	3	2	1	0	1	0	2	5	14
	G	1	2	1	1	5	2	0	5	17
		4	4	2	1	6	2	2	10	31
Tot.	B	484	189	160	127	132	109	75	250	1526
	G	803	233	198	139	151	81	71	306	1982
		1287	422	358	266	283	190	146	556	3508

Referring directly now to Table VII, we find that 44.7 per cent of those not failing the first year do fail later. Of all those who fail the first year, 13.8 per cent escape any later failures. Of all the pupils included in this table 15.8 per cent have 7 or more failures, while of those failing in the first year 27 per cent later have 7 or more failures. For the number included in this table 30.4 per cent have no failures assigned to them.

PERCENTAGE OF FIRST YEAR FAILING GROUPS, WHO LATER HAVE NO FAILURES

No. of F's. in First Year.....	1	2	3	4	5	6	7+
Per Cent of Groups Having no Failures Later.........	18.4	13.7	7.2	9.4	10.5	5.0	12.9

About the same percentage of the boys and of the girls (near 60 per cent) is represented in Table VII. The girls have an advantage over the boys of about 8 per cent for those belonging to the group with no failures, and of about 1 per cent for the group with seven or more failures.

No unconditional conclusion seems justified by this table. In the first year's record of failures there are good grounds for the promise of later performance. We may safely say that those who do not fail the first year are much less likely to fail later, and that if they do fail later, they have less accumulation of failures. Yet some of this group have many failures after the first year, and others who have several failures the first year have none subsequently. Generally, however, the later accumulations are in almost direct ratio to the earlier record, and the later non-failures are in inverse ratio to the debits of the first year.

5. The Prognosis of Failures by the Subject Selection

From the distribution of failures by school subjects as presented in Chapter II, this will seem to be the easiest and almost the surest of all the factors thus far considered to employ for a prognosis of failure. For of all pupils taking Latin we may confidently expect an average of a little less than one pupil in every five to fail each semester. For the entire number taking mathematics, the expectation of failure is an average of about one in six for each semester. German comes next, and for each semester it claims for failure on the average nearly one pupil in every seven taking it. Similarly French claims for failure one in every nine; history, one in every ten; English and business subjects, less than one in every twelve. It will be noted that the average on a semester basis is employed in this part of the computation. Consequently, it is not the same as saying that such a percentage of pupils fail at some time, in the subject. The pupil who fails four times in first year mathematics is intentionally regarded here as representing four failures. Likewise, the pupil who completes four years of Latin without failure represents eight successes for the subject in calculating these percentages. Every recorded failure for each pupil is thus accounted for.

It was also noted in Chapter II that the percentages of the total failures run higher in mathematics, Latin, history, and science, for the graduates than for the non-graduates. This fact is not due to the greater number of failures of graduates in the earlier semesters, when most of the non-graduate failures occur, but to the increase of failures for the graduates in the later years, as is disclosed in Tables II and IV. Accordingly, we may say that those two subjects which are most productive of school failures are increasingly fruitful of such results in the upper years. This does not seem to be the usual or accepted conviction. Certain of the school principals have expressed the assurance that it would be found otherwise. Such deception is easily explainable, for the number of failures show a marked reduction, and the rise of percentages is consequently easily overlooked. It is quite possible, too, that in some individual schools there is not such a rise of the percentages of failure for the graduates in any of the school subjects. In a single one of the eight schools reported here neither Latin nor mathematics showed a higher percentage of failure for the graduate pupils over the non-graduates. In the other seven schools the graduates had the higher percentage in one or both of these subjects.

6. The Time Period and the Number of Failures

The statement that the number of failures will be greater for the failing pupils who remain in school the longer time may seem rather commonplace. But it will not seem trite to state that the percentage of the total failures on the total subject enrollments increases by school semesters up to the seventh; that the percentage of possible failures for all graduating pupils increases likewise; or that the failures per pupil in each single semester tend to increase as the time period extends to the later semesters. Yet radical as these statements may sound, they are actually substantiated by the facts to be presented.

PERCENTAGE OF THE TOTAL FAILURES ON THE TOTAL SUBJECT ENROLLMENT,
BY SEMESTERS

Semester.	1	2	3	4	5	6	7	8	9	10
Per Cent.	11.5	13.9	14.5	15.1	14.5	15.3	12.1	9.9	10.9	6.2

The 808 pupils who received no marks, and many of whom dropped out early in the first semester, are not included in the subject enrollment for the above percentages. Otherwise the enrollments taken are for the beginning of each semester and inclusive of all the pupils. These percentages rise from 11.5 in the first semester to 15.3 in the sixth semester. Then the percentages drop off, doubtless due to the increasing effect by this time of the non-failing graduates on the total enrollment. The graduates alone are next considered in this respect.

PERCENTAGES OF THE TOTAL FAILURES FOR THE GRADUATES ON THE TOTAL
SUBJECT ENROLLMENT FOR GRADUATES, BY SEMESTERS

Semester..	1	2	3	4	5	6	7	8	9	10
Per Cent..	5.9	6.6	7.8	9.1	9.2	10.5	9.1	7.3	8.8	5.2

These percentages are based on the total possibility of failure, and reach their highest point in the sixth semester, where the percentage of failure is nearly twice that for the first semester. These same facts may be effectively presented also by the percentages of such failures for the graduates on the total subject enrollment for only the failing graduates in each semester.

PERCENTAGES OF THE TOTAL FAILURES FOR THE GRADUATES ON THE TOTAL
SUBJECT ENROLLMENT FOR FAILING GRADUATES, BY SEMESTERS

Semester..	1	2	3	4	5	6	7	8	9	10
Per Cent..	31.4	31.2	31.8	32.7	32.3	36.6	37.5	37.4	38.0	36.0

The percentages here are limited to the total possibilities of failure for those graduates who do fail in each semester. They reach the highest point in the ninth semester, with a gradual increase from the first. The high point is reached later in this series than in the one immediately preceding, because while the percentage of pupils failing decreases in the final semesters (p. 14), there is an increase in the number of failures per failing pupil (Table IV).

This increase of percentages by semesters for the graduates on the total possibility of failure, as just noted, is due to an actual increase in the number of failures for the later semesters. By the distribution of failures in Table II more than 56 per cent of the failures are found after the completion of the second year, in spite of the fact that about 10 per cent of the pupils who graduate do so in three or three and a half years. The failures of the graduates are simply the more numerous after the first two years in school. That this situation is no accident due to the superior weight of any single school in the composite group, is readily disclosed by turning to the units which form the composite. For these schools the percentages of the graduates' failures that are found after the second year range from 40 per cent to 66 per cent. In only three of the schools are such percentages under 50 per cent, while in three others they are above 60 per cent.

Further confirmation of how the increase of failures accompanies the pupils who stay longer in school is offered in the facts of Table IV. Here are indicated the number of pupils who before graduating fail 1, 2, 3, etc., times, in semesters 1, 2, 3, etc., up to 10. Of all the occurrences of only one failure per pupil in a semester, 50 per cent are distributed after the fourth semester. In this same period (after the fourth semester) are found 53.2 per cent of those with two failures in a semester; 67.6 per cent of those with three failures in a semester; 71.6 per cent of those having four; 78.6 per cent of those having five; and all of those having six failures in a single semester. One could almost say that the longer they stay the more they fail.

The statements presented herein regarding the relative increase of failures for at least the first three years in school are likely to arouse some surprise among that portion of the people in the profession, with whom the converse of this situation has been quite generally accepted as true. Such an impression has indeed not seemed unwarranted according to some reports, but the responsibility for it must be due in part to the manner of presenting the data, so that at times it actually serves to misstate or to conceal certain important features of the situation. Since the dropping out is heaviest in the early semesters, and since the school undertakes the expense of providing for all who enter, it does not seem to to be a correct presentation of the facts to compute the percentage of failure on only the pupils who finish the whole semester. Such a practice tends to assign an undue percentage of failures to the earlier semesters, one that is considerably too high in comparison with that of the later semesters where the dropping out becomes relatively light. It is not sufficient to report merely what part of our final product is imperfect, instead of reporting, as do most institutions outside of the educational field, what part of all that is taken in becomes waste product. This situation is sufficiently grievous to demand further comment.

In his study of the New Jersey high schools, Bliss states[15] that one of the striking facts found is the "steady decrease of failure from the freshman to the senior year." If we bear in mind that Bliss used only the promotion sheets for his data, and took no account of the drop-outs preceding promotion, and if we then estimate that an average of 10 per cent may drop out before the end of the first semester (the percentage is 13.2 for our eight schools), then the percentages of failure recorded for the first year will be reduced by one-eleventh of their own respective amounts for each school reported by Bliss, as we translate the percentages to the total enrollment basis. As a consequence of such a procedure, Bliss' percentages, as reported for the second year, will be as high as or higher than those for the first year in six of the ten schools concerned, and nearly equal in two more of the schools. It is also evident that his percentages of failure as reported for the junior and senior years are not very different from each other in six of the ten schools, although there is no inclusion of the drop-outs in the percentages stated. The only pronounced or actual decrease in the percentages of failures as Bliss reports them, occurs between the sophomore and junior years, and it is doubtless a significant fact that this decided drop appears at the time and place where the opportunity for elective subjects is first offered in many schools. Yet apparently it has not seemed worth while to most persons who report the facts of failure to compute separately from the other subjects the percentages for the 3- and 4-year required subjects.

A rather small decline is shown in the percentages of failure for the successive semesters, as quoted below for 2,481 high school pupils of Paterson[16] (the average of two semesters), although these percentages are based upon the number of pupils examined at the completion of the semester. It may further be noted that these percentages do not follow the same pupils by semesters, but state the facts for successive classes of pupils. The same criticisms may be offered for the percentages as quoted from Wood[17] for 435 pupils.

PERCENTAGES OF PUPILS FAILING, BY SEMESTERS

SEMESTERS

	1	2	3	4	5	6	7	8
Paterson	17.8	18.4	16.7	15.0	15.6	11.6	9.4	7.4
Wood	24.5	14.5	29.5	30.0	31.0	7.9	16.2	..
OBrien (p. 41)	11.5	13.9	14.5	15.1	14.5	15.3	12.1	9.9

The above series of percentages tend to agree at least in showing little or no decline in the percentages of failure for the first five or six semesters in school.

Another tendency to conceal important features in relation to the facts of school failures may be found in the grouping together of non-continuous and continuous subjects, the latter of which are generally required. F. W. Johnson found in the University of Chicago High School[18] that the percentage of failures by successive years indicated little or no decrease for mathematics and for English (which were 3- and 4-year subjects respectively). The figures were based on the records for a period of two years. In regard to St. Paul, it was possible to compute similar information from the data which were available.[19] The percentages of failure are presented separately in each case for Latin, German, and French, not more than two years of which are required in the schools referred to above. A contrast is thus presented that is both interesting and suggestive.

PERCENTAGES OF PUPILS FAILING, BY YEARS. (Johnson, F. W.)

	YEARS					YEARS			
	1	2	3	4		1	2	3	4
English...	18.1	9.5	18.4	14.4	Latin.....	14.1	9.0	2.9	..
Math.....	12.9	12.9	13.6	5.6	German...	12.4	7.4	..	..
					French...	14.3	9.6	3.1	..

PERCENTAGES OF PUPILS FAILING, BY SEMESTERS. (St. Paul)

	SEMESTERS							
	1	2	3	4	5	6	7	8
English and Math..........	17.8	18.0	16.3	16.9	8.1	14.0	..	..
Latin, German, French.....	17.6	17.5	15.1	7.6	3.0	..	..	..

Apparently the full story has by no means been told when we simply say that there is a general decline in the percentages of failure by years or semesters. First, the failures of the dropouts should be included, so far as it is at all feasible; second, the percentage should be based on the total enrollment in the subject, not on the final product, if we wish to disclose the real situation; third, the continuous or required subjects should be distinguished in order to give a full statement of the facts. On page 41 are presented the percentages of failure for the 1,125 failing graduates alone, as found in this study, the greater portion of whose work, as it actually happened, consisted of 3- and 4-year subjects continuous from the time of entrance, and for whom the percentages of failure increase to the ninth semester.

7. SIMILARITY OF FACTS FOR BOYS AND GIRLS

Nowhere is there any definite indication that any of these factors of prognosis operates more distinctly or more pronouncedly on either boys or girls. Some variations do occur, but differences between the sexes in personal attitudes, social interests, or conventional standards may account for slight differences such as have been already noted. To simplify the statement of facts, no comparison of facts for boys and girls has, in general, been attempted where there was only similarity to be shown.

A SUMMARY OF CHAPTER III

The influence of non-attendance as a factor in school failure is partly provided for here, but no statistical data were secured.

The percentage of physical and mental defects are doubtless comparatively small for high school pupils except in the case of vision.

The facts regarding size of classes were unobtainable

The pupils are distributed by their ages of entrance from 12 to 20, with the mode of the distribution at 15. The younger entering pupils are distinctly more successful in escaping failure. They are also strikingly more successful in their ability to graduate.

The older pupils who fail have a higher percentage of failure on the subjects taken.

The first year's record has real prognostic value for pupils persisting more than three semesters. But 57 per cent of those leaving earlier have no failures. This includes nearly 60 per cent of all the non-failing pupils, but less than 32 per cent of the failing ones have gone that early.

Prediction of failure by subjects is relatively easy and sure, and the later years seem more productive of this result.

The percentage of failure on the total possibility of failure increases with the time period up to the seventh semester. The same facts are true for the graduates when considered alone. Fifty-six per cent of the failures for the graduates occur after the second year. The longer stay in school actually begets an increase of failures. The boys and girls are similarly affected by these factors of prognosis.

REFERENCES

1. Keyes, C. H. *Progress Through the Grades*, pp. 23, 62.
2. Terman, L. M. *The Measurement of Intelligence*, p. 68.
3. Bronner, A. E. *Psychology of Special Abilities and Disabilities*.
4. Ayres, L. P. " The Effect of Physical Defects on School Progress," *Psychological Clinic*, 3:71.
5. Gulick, L. H., Ayres, L. P. *Medical Inspection in the Schools*, p. 194.
6. *Standards of The North Central Association of Colleges and Secondary Schools*.
7. Hall-Quest, A. L., in Johnson's *Modern High School*, p. 270.
8. King, I. *The High School Age*, p. 195.
9. VanDenburg, J. K. *The Elimination of Pupils from Public Secondary Schools*, p. 113.
10. Slattery, M. *The Girl in Her Teens*, p. 20.
11. Wooley, H. T. " Facts About the Working Children of Cincinnati," *Elementary School Teacher*, 14:135.

12. *Report of Commission on Industrial and Technical Education* (Mass.), 1906, p. 92.

13. Barrows, Alice P. *Report of Vocational Guidance Survey* (New York City), Public Education Association, New York City, Bull. No. 9, 1912.

14. Holley, C. E. *The Relationship Between Persistence in School and Home Conditions*, Fifteenth Yearbook, Pt. II, p. 98.

15. Bliss, D. C. " High School Failures," *Educational Administration and Supervision*, Vol. III.

16. *Annual Report of Board of Education, Paterson*, 1915.

17. Wood, J. W. " A Study of Failures," *School and Society*, I, 679.

18. Johnson, F. W. " A Study of High School Grades," *School Review*, 19-13.

19. Strayer, G. D., Coffman, L. D., Prosser, C. A. *Report of a Survey of the School System of St. Paul*, 1917.

CHAPTER IV

HOW MUCH IS THE GRADUATION OR THE PERSISTENCE IN SCHOOL CONDITIONED BY THE OCCURRENCE OR THE NUMBER OF FAILURES?

1. COMPARISON OF THE FAILING AND THE NON-FAILING GROUPS IN REFERENCE TO GRADUATION AND PERSISTENCE

It has been noted in section 1 of Chapter II that 58.1 per cent of all the graduates have school failures. Here we mean to carry the analysis and comparison in reference to graduation and failure somewhat further. To this end the following distribution is significant.

DISTRIBUTION OF PUPILS IN REFERENCE TO FAILURE AND GRADUATION

	The Non-failing Pupils—Graduating		The Failing Pupils—Graduating	
Totals.......	2568	811 (31.5%)	3573	1125 (31.5%)
Boys........	1001	307 (30.6%)	1645	489 (29.7%)
Girls........	1567	504 (32.1%)	1928	639 (33.0%)

We have presented here the numbers that graduate without failures, together with the total group to which they belong, and the same for the graduates who have failed. By a mere process of subtraction we may determine the number of non-graduates, as well as the number of these that fail, and then compute the percentage of the non-graduates who fail. Thus we get 58.2 per cent (boys—62.5, girls—54.9) as the percentage of the non-graduates failing. It is apparent at once that this is almost identical with the percentage of failure for the ones who graduate (Chapter II), but for the non-graduates the boys and girls are a little further apart. It may be remarked in this connection that no effort was made to include any of the 808 non-credited pupils among the ones who fail. The inclusion of 60 per cent of this number as potentially failing pupils, as was done in Chapter II, will raise the above percentage of failing non-graduates by 11.5 per cent.

48

The above distribution of pupils enables us to determine what percentage of the failing and of the non-failing groups graduate. These percentages are identical—31.5 per cent in each case. The boys and girls are further apart in the former group (boys—29.7, girls—33) than in the latter group (boys—30.6, girls—32.1). It follows, then, that the percentage who graduate of all the original entrants is 31.5 per cent. This fact varies by schools from 20.8 per cent to 45.4 per cent. And such percentage is in each case exclusive of the pupils who join the class by transfers from other schools or classes. Our particular interest is not in how many pupils the school graduates in any year, but rather in how many of the entering pupils in any one year stay to graduate.

The greater persistence of the failing non-graduates, or the greater failing for the more persistent non-graduates, has already been given some attention in both Chapters II and III. In the following distribution the non-graduates alone are considered. The number persisting in school to each succeeding semester is first stated, and then the percentage of that number which is composed of the non-failing pupils is given.

DISTRIBUTION OF THE NON-GRADUATES ACCORDING TO THE NUMBERS PERSISTING TO EACH SUCCESSIVE SEMESTER

BY END OF SEMESTERS

	1	2	3	4	5	6	7	8	9	10
Total (4205)....	2787	1957	1572	999	761	390	234	60	23	4
Per Cent of Non-failing (41.8)..	24.5	20.0	16.4	13.9	12.7	7.2	3.8	1.6	0	..

Only 20 per cent of the non-graduates who remain to the end of the first year (second semester) do not fail. Although the failing non-graduates outnumber the non-failing ones when all the pupils who finally drop out are considered, their percentage of the majority increases rapidly for each successive semester continued in school. That the non-failing non-graduates are in general not the ones who persist long in school is shown by these percentages.

2. THE NUMBER OF FAILURES AND THE YEARS TO GRADUATE

The following table shows how the number of failures are related to the time period required for graduation. The distribution in Table VIII shows a range from 1 to 25 failures per pupil, and a time period for graduation ranging from 3 to 6 years. It is evident from this distribution that the increase of

TABLE VIII

DISTRIBUTION OF PUPILS GRADUATING, ACCORDING TO THE TOTAL FAILURES EACH AND THE TIME TAKEN TO GRADUATE

NO. OF FAILURES		3	$3\frac{1}{2}$	4	$4\frac{1}{2}$	5	$5\frac{1}{2}$	6	TOTALS
0	Boys........	20	23	244	12	8	..	..	307
	Girls........	54	26	380	30	14	..	..	504
1	Boys........	2	10	59	7	2	..	..	80
	Girls........	5	8	83	13	5	..	..	114
2	Boys........	2	2	64	7	7	0	..	82
	Girls........	2	3	88	11	8	1	..	113
3	Boys........	0	6	27	5	4	..	..	42
	Girls........	1	1	53	6	3	..	..	64
4	Boys........	1	1	44	0	8	1	..	55
	Girls........	4	6	57	8	4	1	..	80
5	Boys........	0	1	41	2	3	..	..	47
	Girls........	1	2	26	7	5	..	..	41
6	Boys........	..	0	29	6	3	..	0	38
	Girls........	..	1	29	3	8	..	1	42
7	Boys........	..	2	12	7	7	..	..	28
	Girls........	..	1	13	4	5	..	..	23
8	Boys........	..	0	17	7	8	..	1	33
	Girls........	..	1	16	9	7	..	0	33
9	Boys........	..	0	6	5	5	0	0	16
	Girls........	..	1	7	8	8	1	1	26
10	Boys........	..	1	6	4	6	0	..	17
	Girls........	..	1	14	5	2	1	..	23
11-15	Boys........	..	0	9	18	11	0	1	39
	Girls........	..	1	11	25	14	1	4	56
16-20	Boys........	..	..	2	2	4	1	1	10
	Girls........	..	..	2	5	2	2	0	11
21-25	Boys........	..	..	1	0	0	1	0	2
	Girls........	..	..	0	1	4	3	1	9
Total	Boys........	25	46	561	82	76	3	3	796
	Girls........	67	52	780	135	89	10	7	1140

time period for graduating is not commensurate with the number of failures for the individual. By far the largest number graduate in four years in spite of their numerous failures. Nearly 70 per cent of the failing graduates require four years or less for graduation. The number who finish in three years is greater than the number who require either five and one-half or six years. The median number of failures per pupil is 4. The pupils with fewer than 4 failures who take more than four years to graduate are not representative of any particular school in this composite, nor are those having 10 or more failures who take less than 5 years to graduate.

In reading Table VIII, we find that 20 boys and 54 girls who have no failures graduate in three years; 2 boys and 5 girls fail once and graduate in 3 years; 10 boys and 8 girls have one failure and graduate in 3½ years, and so on. The median period is 4 years for those with no failures and it remains at 4 for all who have fewer than 9 failures; but the median time period is not above 5 years for the highest number of failures.

3. The Number of Failures and the Semester of Dropping Out for the Non-graduates

The pages preceding this point have given evidence that the failing pupils are not mainly the ones who drop out early. But we may still ask whether the number of failures per individual tends to determine how early he will be eliminated? This question calls for the facts of the next table. In this table the semesters of dropping out are indicated at the top. The failures range as high as 25 per pupil, and it is evident that not all pupils have left school until the eleventh semester. The distribution includes the 1156 boys and the 1292 girls who failed and did not graduate; also the 694 boys and the 1063 girls who dropped out without failing. The wide distribution of these non-graduates, both relative to the number of failures and to the time of dropping out, is forcibly brought to our attention by the table which follows.

TABLE IX

DISTRIBUTION OF THE NON-GRADUATES, ACCORDING TO THE TOTAL FAILURES EACH AND THE TIME OF DROPPING OUT

NO. OF FAILURES		SEMESTER OF DROPPING OUT											TOTAL
		1	2	3	4	5	6	7	8	9	10	11	
0	B.	430	134	40	41	15	24	7	3	0	..	..	694
	G.	643	163	89	78	27	45	12	5	1	..	..	1063
													1757
1	B.	35	53	25	33	14	9	1	1	..	..	..	171
	G.	46	65	25	34	12	12	4	3	..	..	..	201
													372
2	B.	52	58	18	30	8	17	5	6	..	..	..	194
	G.	49	79	31	36	12	17	3	3	..	..	..	230
													424
3	B.	43	41	22	28	9	10	5	1	0	..	..	159
	G.	54	52	19	34	18	17	0	6	1	..	..	201
													360
4	B.	27	31	13	32	7	11	9	2	..	..	..	132
	G.	34	43	23	29	11	16	5	8	..	..	..	169
													301
5	B.	3	13	14	30	11	16	11	4	..	..	..	102
	G.	2	14	18	24	5	13	3	5	..	..	..	84
													186
6	B.	..	27	8	24	11	16	11	6	0	0	..	103
	G.	..	17	14	25	10	11	3	9	2	1	..	92
													195
7	B.	..	8	7	7	6	16	5	3	0	1	..	53
	G.	..	9	3	15	8	7	5	5	0	0	..	52
													105
8	B.	..	8	3	14	6	11	6	5	1	0	..	54
	G.	..	10	5	15	7	10	6	6	1	1	..	61
													115
9	B.	..	1	1	7	5	8	2	7	3	1	..	35
	G.	..	0	2	7	8	9	2	4	1	0	..	33
													68
10	B.	..	2	2	10	2	7	6	10	0	..	..	39
	G.	..	2	1	6	5	9	4	4	0	..	..	31
													70
11-15	B.	..	..	1	8	7	27	14	22	5	2	0	86
	G.	..	..	1	5	12	22	20	23	9	6	2	100
													186
16-20	B.	..	..	..	1	0	8	3	6	3	3	0	24
	G.	..	..	..	0	2	3	3	12	6	2	2	30
													54
21-25	B.	..	..	..	..	..	..	..	2	1	1	..	4
	G.	..	..	..	..	..	..	1	3	3	1	..	8
													12
TOTAL	B.	590	376	154	265	101	180	85	78	13	8	0	1850
	G.	828	454	231	308	137	191	71	96	24	11	4	2355
													4205

Table IX reads in a manner similar to Table VIII: 430 boys and 643 girls, having 0 failures, drop out in the first semester; 35 boys and 46 girls drop out in the first semester with a single failure; 3 boys and 2 girls drop out in the first semester with five failures each.

For a small portion of these drop-outs the number of failures is undoubtedly the prime or immediate factor in securing their elimination. It seems probable that such is the situation for most of those pupils who drop out after 50 per cent or more of their school work has resulted in failures. Yet a few of these pupils manage to continue for an extended time in school, as the following distribution shows.

DROP-OUTS FAILING IN 50 PER CENT OR MORE OF THEIR TOTAL WORK, AND THEIR DISTRIBUTION BY SEMESTERS OF DROPPING OUT

				SEMESTERS					
1	2	3	4	5	6	7	8	9	10
221 B 81	69	17	24	7	15	4	2	1	1
264 G 98	68	20	35	14	10	5	8	5	1
%of Total 36.9	28.2	7.6	12.2	4.3	5.2	1.9	2.0	1.2	.4

This grouping includes 485 pupils, or 11.5 per cent of the total number of 4,205 drop-outs. But whatever the part may be that is played by failing it is evident that it does not operate to cause their early loss to the school in nearly all of these instances. It may be noted here that it is difficult to find any justification for allowing or forcing these pupils to endure two, three, or four years of a kind of training for which they have shown themselves obviously unfitted. To be sure, they have satisfied a part of these failures by repetitions or otherwise, but only to go on adding more failures. A device of 'super-annuation' is employed in certain schools by which a pupil who has failed in half of his work for two semesters, and is sixteen years of age, is supposed to be dropped automatically from the school. This device seems designed to evade a difficulty in the absence of any real solution for it, and harmonizes with the school aims that are prescribed in terms of subject matter rather than in terms of the pupils' needs. From the standpoint of the individual pupil his peculiar qualities are not likely to be fashioned to the highest degree of usefulness by this procedure. It simply serves notice that the pupil must make the adjustment needed, as the school cannot or will not.

Notwithstanding the testimony furnished by the accumulation of failures shown in Table IX, there are grounds for believing that for the major portion of all the non-graduates the number of failures is not a prime nor perhaps a highly important cause of their dropping out of school. This conviction seems to be substantiated by the statement of percentages below.

The Percentage of Non-Graduates Who Drop Out With

0 Failure	1 or 0 Failure	2 or fewer Failures	3 or fewer Failures	4 or fewer Failures	5 or fewer Failures
41.8	50.6	60.7	69.2	76.4	80.8

The fact that nearly 81 per cent of the non-graduates have only 5 failures or less, taken in comparison with the fact that approximately one fourth of the failing graduates have 8 or more failures, argues that the number of failures alone can hardly be considered one of the larger factors in causing the dropping out. In a report concerning the working children of Cincinnati, H. T. Wooley remarks[1] that "two-thirds of our children leaving the public schools are the failures." This seems to suppose failing a large cause of the dropping out. But this investigation of failure indicates that the percentage of failure for those leaving is no higher than for the ones who do not leave. A similar illustration is credited to O. W. Caldwell[2], who makes reference to the large percentage of the failing pupils who leave high school, without taking any recognition of the equally large percentage of the failing pupils who continue in the high school.

There is in no sense any intention here to condone the large number of failures simply because it is pointed out that they do not operate chiefly to cause elimination from school. The above facts may lead to some such conviction as that expressed by Wooley,[1] after giving especial attention to those who had left school, that "the real force that is sending a majority of these children out into the industrial field is their own desire to go to work, and behind this desire is frequently the dissatisfaction with school." A somewhat similar conviction seems to be shared by King,[3] in saying that "the pupil who yields unwillingly to the narrow round of school tasks . . . will grasp at almost any pretext to quit school." W. F. Book tabulated the reasons why pupils leave high school,[4] as given by 1,051 pupils. He found that discouragement, loss of interest, and disappointment affect more pupils than all the other causes combined. Likewise

Bronner notes[5] that the 'irrational' sameness of school procedure for all pupils often leads to "serious loss of interest in school work, discouragement, truancy, and disciplinary problems." Still it may be that the worst consequences of multiplied failures are not to those dropping out. W. D. Lewis observes[6] that the failing pupil "speedily comes to accept himself as a failure," and that "the disaster to many who stay in the schools is greater than to those who are shoved out." To the same point Hanus tells[7] us that "during the school period aversion and evasion are more frequently cultivated than power and skill, through the forced pursuit of uninteresting subjects." A pupil who acquires the habit of failing and the attitude of accepting it as a necessary evil may soon give up trying to win and become satisfied to accept himself as less gifted, or even to accept life in general as necessarily a matter of repeated failures. In a similar connection, James E. Russell says,[8] "the boy who becomes accustomed to second place soon fails to think at his best." Such psychological results in regard to habits and attitude accruing from repeated failures are both certain and insidious. And an education which purports to be for all and to offer the highest training to each must abandon the inculcation of attitudes of mind so detrimental to the individual and to the very society which educates him.

4. THE PERCENTAGES THAT THE NON-GRADUATE GROUPS FORM OF THE PUPILS WHO HAVE EACH SUCCESSIVELY HIGHER NUMBER OF FAILURES

By merely adding the columns of totals for Tables VIII and IX, we are able to obtain the full number of pupils who have each number of failures from 1 to 25. We may readily secure the percentages for the non-graduates in each of these groups by referring again to the numbers in the totals column of Table IX. The following series of percentages are thus obtained.

THE PERCENTAGE FORMED BY NON-GRADUATES WITH 0, 1, 2, 3, ETC., FAILURES ON THE TOTAL NUMBER WHO HAVE 0, 1, 2, 3, ETC., FAILURES

No. of Failures.	0	1	2	3	4	5	6	7	8
Per Cent	68.4	65.7	68.5	77.2	69.0	68.0	70.6	67.3	63.5

No. of Failures.	9	10	11	12	13	14	15	16	17+
Per Cent	61.8	63.6	69.0	61.2	66.0	65.3	70.0	61.5	69.4

That these percentages would be higher for the non-graduates than for the graduates (that is, above 50 per cent) would certainly be expected by a glance at their higher numbers in every group of their distribution. But it would hardly be expected by most of us that the percentages would show no general tendency to rise as the failures per pupil increase in number, yet such is the truth as found here. The reverse of these facts was found by Aaron I. Dotey, with a smaller group of high school pupils[9] (1,397), studied in one of the New York City high schools. Still he also asserts that failure in studies is not a cause of elimination to the extent that it is generally supposed to be. We may gain some advantage for judging the general tendency of the extended and varied series of percentages above, by computing them in groups of larger size, thus yielding a briefer series, as follows:

(A CONDENSED FORM OF THE PRECEDING STATEMENT)

No. of Failures...	0	1 to 4	5 to 8	9 to 12	13 to 16	17 to 25
Per Cent........	68.4	67.6	67.3	63.9	65.7	69.4

Not only do the percentages of non-graduates not increase relatively as the numbers of failure go higher, but there is a slight general decline in these percentages until we reach '17 or more' failures per pupil. Then for '17 to 25' failures per pupil there is an increase of only 1 per cent over that for 0 failures. The number of failures does not seem directly to condition the pupil's ability to graduate or to continue to in school.

5. TIME EXTENSION FOR THE FAILING GRADUATES

We shall now inquire further what extension of time for graduating characterizes the failing graduates in comparison with the non-failing ones.

The distribution according to the period for graduation for the 1,936 pupils who graduate was shown by the summary lines of Table VIII. In the same table the non-failing graduates are included (but distinct). No pupil graduates in less than three years and none takes longer than six years; 9.8 per cent of the number finish in less than 4 years; 19.7 per cent take more than 4 years. The small number that finish earlier than four years may be due in part to the single annual graduation in several of the schools. Some of the schools admitting two classes each year graduated only one, and the records made it plain that some pupils had a half year more credit than was needed for graduating. Considering, however, that about 42 per cent of the graduates had no failures, they should have been able to speed up more on the time period of getting through. They were doubtless not unable to do that. But some principals hold the conviction that four years will result in a rounding out of the pupil more than commensurate with the extended time. More than 35 per cent of those who did finish in less than four years are graduates who had failed from 1 to 11 times. In the conventional period of four years 77 per cent of the non-failing and 64 per cent of the failing graduates complete their work and graduate (see p. 59, for the means employed). The percentages of non-failing graduates for each time period are given below.

THE PERCENTAGES OF NON-FAILING GRADUATES FOR EACH PERIOD

Time Period in Years.....	3	$\frac{1}{2}$	4	$\frac{1}{2}$	5	$\frac{1}{2}$	6
Per Cent of Non-Failing..	80.4	50.0	46.5	19.3	13.3	..	..

This continuous decline of percentages representing the non-failing graduates shows that they have an evident advantage in regard to the time period for graduating. Their percentages are high for the shorter time periods and low for the longer periods. But by reference to Table VIII we quickly find that the slight extension of the time period for the failing graduates is not at all commensurate with the number of failures which they have. The failures are provided for in various ways, as Chapter V will explain. No striking differences are observed for the boys and girls in any division of this chapter.

A SUMMARY OF CHAPTER IV

The percentages of graduates and of non-graduates that fail are almost identical.

The percentages of the failing pupils who graduate and of the non-failing pupils who graduate are identical (31.5 per cent); hence, graduation is not perceptibly conditioned by the occurrence of failure.

The non-failing non-graduates do not persist long in school, as compared with the failing non-graduates. The short persistence partly accounts for their avoidance of failure.

As the number of failures per pupil increase for the failing graduates, the time extension is not commensurate with the number of failures.

For 11.5 per cent of the non-graduates who fail in 50 per cent or more of their work, failure is probably a chief cause of dropping out.

Failure is probably not a prime cause of dropping out for most of the non-graduates, as 80 per cent have only 5 failures or fewer.

The worst consequences of failure are perhaps in acquiring the habit of failing, and in coming to accept one's self as a failure. The number of drop-outs does not tend to increase as the number of failures per pupil increases.

The time period for graduating ranges from three to six years, with approximately 79 per cent of all graduates finishing in four years or less. The failing graduates take, on the average, a little longer time than the non-failing, but not an increase that is proportionate to the number of failures.

The boys and girls present no striking differences in the facts of Chapter IV.

REFERENCES :

1. Wooley, H. T. "Facts About the Working Children of Cincinnati," *Elementary School Teacher*, Vol. XIV, 135.
2. Caldwell, O. W. "Laboratory Method and High School Efficiency," *Popular Science Monthly*, 82-243.
3. King, Irving. *The High School Age.*
4. Book, W. F. "Why Pupils Fail," *Pedagogical Seminary*, 11:204.
5. Bronner, A. E. *The Psychology of Special Abilities and Disabilities*, p. 6.
6. Lewis, W. D. *Democracy's High School*, pp. 28, 37.
7. Hanus, P. H. *School Aims and Values.*
8. Russell, J. E. "Co-education in High School. Is It a Failure?" Reprint from *Good Housekeeping.*
9. Dotey, A. I. *An Investigation of Scholarship Records of High School Pupils.* High School Teachers Association of New York City. Bulletins 1911-14, p. 220.

CHAPTER V

ARE THE SCHOOL AGENCIES EMPLOYED IN REMEDYING FAILURES ADEQUATE FOR THE PURPOSE?

The caption of this chapter suggests the inquiry as to what are the agencies employed by the school for this purpose, and how extensively does each function? The different means employed and the number attempting in the various ways to satisfy for the failures charged are classified and stated below, but the success of each method is considered later in its turn. One might think also of time extension, night school, summer school, correspondence courses, and tutoring as possible factors deserving to be included here in the list of remedies for failures made. The matter of time extension has already been partly treated in Chapter IV, while the facts for the other agencies mentioned are rather uncertain and difficult to trace on the records. However, they all tend to eventuate finally in one of the methods noted below.

The Disposition Made of the School Failures

Total No. Failures	Repeat the Subject	School Final or Spec.	Exam. Regents' Exam's.	Discon. or Substitution	Contin. Repet. or Exam.	Both No Repeat and Exam.
8348 B..	3695	821	1333	2471	259	231
9612 G..	5001	1025	1752	1929	249	344
Per Cent of Total	48.4	10.3	17.2	24.5	2.8	3.2

It is obvious from these percentages that school practice puts an inclusive faith in the repetition of the subject, as 48.4 per cent of all the failures are referred to this one remedy for the purpose of being rectified, although one school made practically no use of this means (see section 5 of this chapter). We shall proceed to find how effectively it operates and how much this faith is warranted by the results. The cases above designated as

59

both repeating and taking examination (3.2 per cent) have been counted twice, and their percentage must be subtracted from the sum of the percentages in order to give 100 per cent.

1. Repetition as a Remedy for Failures

We already know how many of the failing pupils repeat the subject of failure, but the success attending such repetition is entitled to further attention. Accordingly, the grades received in the 8,696 repetitions are presented here.

Grades Secured in the Subjects Repeated

| Total Repetitions | GRADES | | | | |
	A	B	C	D	Inc.
3695 Boys....................	63	547	1863	1003	219
5001 Girls....................	83	724	2510	1337	347
Per Cent of Total..............	1.7	14.7	50.3	33.3	

Less than 2 per cent of the repeaters secure A's, while only about 1 in 6 ever secures either an A or a B. The first three are passing grades, with values as explained in Chapter I, and D represents failure. Of the repeated subjects 33.3 per cent result in either a D or an unfinished status. It is a fair assumption that the unfinished grade usually bore pretty certain prospects of being a failing grade if completed, and it is so treated here. There is a difference of less than 1 per cent in the failures assigned to boys and girls for the repeated subjects.

The hope was entertained in the original plan of this study to secure several other sorts of information about the repeaters, but these later proved to be unobtainable. The influence of repeating with the same teacher as contrasted with a change of teachers in the same subject, the comparative facts for the repetition with men or with women teachers, the varying results for the different sizes of classes, and the apparent effect of supervised study of some sort before or after failing, were all sought for in the records available; but the schools were not able to provide any definite and complete information of the sorts here specified.

a. *Size of Schedule and Results of Repeating*

It would seem plausible that the failing pupils who were permitted and who possessed the energy would want to take one or more extra subjects to balance the previous loss of credit due to failure. Then it becomes important at once for the administrative head to know whether the proportion of failures bears a definite relationship to the size of the pupil's schedule of subjects. A normal schedule for most purposes and for most of the schools includes, on the average, four subjects or twenty weekly hours, In this study the schedule which each individual school claimed as normal schedule, has been accepted as such, all larger schedules being considered extra size and all smaller ones reduced. For instance, in one of the schools five subjects are considered a normal schedule even though they totaled 24 points, which is not usual. But in the other schools a normal schedule includes the range from 18 to 22 points irrespective of those carried in the subjects outside of the classification included in this study; while above 22 points is an extra schedule and below 18 a reduced schedule in the same sense as above. For the most part this meant that five or more of such subjects form an extra schedule, and that three form a reduced schedule. In this manner all the repeated subjects are classed as part of a reduced, a normal, or an extra sized schedule as follows.

Size of Schedules for Pupils Taking Repeated Subjects

Total	Reduced	Normal	Extra
3695 Boys	132	1762	180ɪ
5001 Girls	164	2684	2153
Per Cent of Total	3.4	51.1	45.5

This distribution indicates that relatively few of the pupils take a reduced schedule in repeating. For the succeeding comparison with the grades of extra schedule pupils, those having a normal or reduced schedule are grouped together.

Grades for Subjects Repeated by Failing Pupils Who Carried a Reduced or Normal Schedule

Total Repetitions	A	B	C	D	..
1894 Boys	34	259	894	541	166
2848 Girls	44	361	1319	840	284
Per Cent of Total	1.6	13.1	46.7	38.6	

In this distribution are the grades for 4742 instances of repetition. Of these, 38.6 per cent fail to pass after repeating. It is not possible to say definitely how many of these pupils actually determine their schedule by a free choice, and how many are restricted by school authorities or by home influence. But certain it is that a policy of opposition exists in some schools and with some teachers to allowing repeaters to carry more than a prescribed schedule; and in most schools at least some form of discrimination or regulation is exercised in this matter. It will appear from the next distribution that a rule of uniformity in regard to size of schedule, without regard to the individual pupils, is here, as elsewhere, lacking in wisdom and is in disregard of the facts.

Grades for the Subjects Repeated, with an Extra Schedule

Total Repetitions	A	B	C	D	
1801 Boys	29	288	969	462	53
2153 Girls	39	363	1191	497	63
Per Cent of Total	1.7	16.6	54.5	27.2	

Out of the 3,954 repeated subjects in this distribution, 72.8 per cent secure passing grades, 27.2 per cent result in failures. This means that the repeaters with an extra schedule have 11.4 per cent fewer failing grades than the repeaters who carry only a normal or a reduced schedule. They also excel in the percentage of A's and B's secured for repeated subjects. In only one of the eight schools was the reverse of these general facts found to be true. In one other school the difference was more than 2 to 1 in favor of the extra schedule repeaters as judged by the percentages of failure for each group. It seems that at least three factors operate to secure superior results for repeaters with heavier schedule. First, they are undoubtedly a more highly selected group in reference to ability and energy. Second, they have the advantage of the spur and the motivation which comes from the consciousness of a heavier responsibility, and from which emanates greater earnestness of effort. Third, it is probable that some teachers are more helpful and considerate in the aiding and grading of pupils who appear to be working hard. It is, at any rate, a plain fact that those who are willing and who are permitted to take extra work are the more successful. Excessive emphasis must not be placed on the latter requirement alone, as willingness frequently seems to be the only essential condition imposed.

b. Later Grades in the Same Kind of Subjects, Following Repetition and Without It

Next in importance to the degree of success attending the repetition of failing subjects is the effect which such repetition has upon the results in later subjects of the same kind. By tabulating separately the later grades in like subjects for those who had repeated and for those who had not repeated after failure, we have the basis for the following comparison of results. It should be stated at this point that by the same kind of subject is not meant a promiscuous grouping together of all language or of all history courses. But for languages a later course in the same language is implied, with the single exception that Latin and French are treated as though French were a mere continuation of the Latin preceding it. Certain other decisions are as arbitrary. Greek, Roman, and ancient history are considered as in the same class; so are modern, English, and American history. The general and the biological sciences are grouped together, but the physical sciences are distinguished as a separate group. The various commercial subjects are considered to be of the same kind only when they are the same subject. All mathematics subjects are regarded as the same kind of subjects except commercial arithmetic which is classed as a commercial subject. All the later marks given in what was regarded as the same kind of subject, are included in the two distributions of grades which follow.

LATER GRADES IN THE SAME KIND OF SUBJECT, AFTER FAILURE AND REPE-
TITION OF THE SUBJECT

Total	A	B	C	D
2788 Boys	28	308	1441	1011
3489 Girls	33	307	1748	1401
Per Cent of Total	.9	9.8	50.8	38.4

This distribution shows a marked tendency for failures in any subject to be accompanied by further failures (38.4 per cent), not only in the subjects for which it is a prerequisite but in subjects closely akin to it. If this tendency to succeeding failures is really dependent upon thoroughness in the preceding subject, then the repetition of the subject should offer an opportunity for greater thoroughness and should prove to be a distinct advantage in this regard.   When we compare the percentage of failures above with that in the following distribution, we fail to find evidence of such an advantage in repetition.   The continuity of failures by subjects and the ineffectiveness of repetition are pointed out by T. H. Briggs[1] as found in an unpublished study by J. H. Riley, showing that after repeating and passing the subjects of failure, 33 per cent of those who continued the subject failed again the next semester.

ATER GRADES IN THE SAME KIND OF SUBJECTS, F OLLOWING FAILURE BUT WITH NO REPETITION

Total	A	B	C	D
1269 Boys	5	102	639	523
1191 Girls	8	147	669	367
Per Cent of Total	.5	10.1	53.1	36.2

Here the same pronounced tendency is disclosed for the occurrence of other subsequent failures in the subjects closely similar. But for this distribution of grades, secured without any preceding repetitions, the unsuccessful result is 2.2 per cent lower than that found for those who had repeated.   This group is not so large in numbers as the one above, and undoubtedly there is some distinct element of pupil selection involved, for it is not easy to believe that the repetition should work a positive injury to the later grades.   Nevertheless, our faith in the worth of unconditional repetitions should properly be disturbed by such disclosures.

c. *The Grades in Repeated Subjects and in the New Work, for the Same Semester and the Same Pupils*

If it is granted that the teachers of the repeaters are equally good as compared with the others, then the previous familiarity with the work that is being repeated might be expected to serve as an advantage in its favor when compared with the new and advanced work in other subjects.   But the grades for the new and advanced work as presented below, and the grades for the repeated subjects as presented earlier in this chapter (section 1), deny the validity of such an assumption and give us a different version of the facts.

THE GRADES SECURED IN NEW WORK, AT SAME TIME AND BY SAME PUPILS
AS THE GRADES SECURED IN THE REPEATED SUBJECTS

Total	A	B	C	D
11,029 Boys	256	2225	5543	3005
11,941 Girls	198	2064	6604	3075
Per Cent of Total	1.9	18.6	53.1	26.4

The facts not only show a lower percentage (by 6.9 per cent) of unsuccessful grades in the new work, but they also show a higher percentage of A's, of B's, and of C's than for the repeated subjects. There is definite suggestion here that often the particular subject of failure may be more responsible and more at fault than the particular pupil. Certainly uniformity and an arbitrary routine of tasks ignore the individual differences of interests and abilities. But by their greater and their repeated failures in the same deficient subjects (see p. 66) these pupils seem to have reasserted stoutly the facts ignored. They have been asked to repeat and repeat again subjects which they have already indicated their unfitness to handle successfully. This pursuance of an unsuccessful method is not good procedure in the business world. The doctor does not employ such methods.

d. The Number and Results of Identical Repetitions

It has become apparent before this that some pupils fail several times and in identical subjects because of their unsuccessful repetitions after each failure. Final success might at times justify multiplied repetitions, but in such instances it becomes increasingly important that the repetition should eventually end in success after the subject has been repeated two, three or four times. If such is not the result, then the method is at best a misdirection of energy; or still worse it is an irreparable error, expensive to the individual and the school alike, which only serves to accentuate the inequalities and perversions of opportunity imposed by an arbitrary requirement of the same subjects, the same methods, and the same scheme of education for all pupils alike, regardless of their capacities and interests. In using the term identical it is intended to designate just one unit of the course, as English I, or Latin II. The following table will disclose the facts as to the success resulting from each number of such successive and identical repetitions per pupil.

TABLE X

THE NUMBERS AND RESULTS OF REPEATED REPETITIONS, FOR IDENTICAL SUBJECTS

NO. OF REPET.		A	B	Grades C	D	No Grade	Totals	Per Cent Failing
1	Boys	62	532	1727	880	216	3417	
	Girls	80	702	2329	1180	342	4633	32.5
2	Boys	1	15	106	77	3	202	
	Girls	3	17	154	89	2	265	36.6
3	Boys	..	0	26	33	0	59	
	Girls	..	5	19	36	3	63	59.0
4	Boys	..	..	4	11	..	15	
	Girls	..	..	8	25	..	33	75.0
5	Boys	..	..	..	2	..	2	
	Girls	..	..	..	5	..	5	100.0
6	Boys	..	..	..	0	..	0	
	Girls	..	..	..	2	..	2	100.0
Tot.	Boys	63	547	1863	1003	219	3695	
	Girls	83	724	2510	1337	347	5001	

Although a smaller number of pupils make each higher number of repetitions, a higher percentage of each successive group meets with final failure in the subject repeated, and the facts are indicative of what should be expected however large the numbers making such multiplied repetitions. It seems almost incredible that pupils should anywhere be required or permitted to make the fourth, fifth, or sixth repetition of subjects so manifestly certain of leading to further disappointment. It must be understood, too, that five and six repetitions means six and seven times over the same school work. The existence of such a situation testifies to a sort of deep-seated faith in the dependence of the pupil's educational salvation on the successful repetiton of some particular school subject. It shows no recognition that the duty of the school is to give each pupil the type of training best suited to his individual endowments and limitations, and at the same time in keeping with the needs of society. Such indiscriminate repetition becomes a matter of thoughtless duplicating and operates, first, to increase the economic, educational, and human waste, where the school is especially the agency charged with conserving the greatest of our national resources. Second, it operates to fix more permanently the habit and attitude of failing for such pupils, and bequeaths to society the fruit of such maladjustments, which cannot fail to function frequently and seriously in the production of industrial dissatisfactions and misfits later in life. Such probabilities are merely in keeping with the psychological fact that habits once established are not likely to be easily lost. Indiscriminate repetition is an expensive way of failing to do the thing which it assumes to do.

Surely one finds in the preceding pages rather slight grounds to warrant the almost unqualified faith in repetition such as the school practice exhibits (Table X), or in the importance of the particular subjects so repeated. There may be evidence in this faith and practice of what Snedden[2] calls the " undue importance attached to the historic instruments of secondary education . . . now taught mainly because of the ease with which they can be presented . . . and which may have had little distinguishable bearing on the future achievement of those young people so gifted by nature as to render it probable that they should later become leaders." But such instruments will not lack direct bearing on the productions of failures for pupils whose interests and needs are but remotely served by such subjects.

A recent ruling in the department of secondary education,[3] in New York City, denies high school pupils permission " to repeat the same grade and type of work for the third consecutive time " after failing a second time. And further it is prescribed that " students who have failed twice in any given grade of a foreign language should be dropped from all classes in that language." Our findings in this study will seem to verify the wisdom of these rulings. Another ruling that " students who have failed to complete successfully four prepared subjects should not be permitted to elect more than four in the succeeding term," or if they " have passed four subjects and failed in one," should be permitted to take five only provisionally, seems to judge the individual's capacities pretty much in terms of failure. We have found that for approximately 4,000 repetitions with an extra schedule, however or by whomever they may have been determined, the percentage getting A's and B's was higher and the percentage of failing was substantially lower than for approximately 4,700 repetitions with only three or four subjects 'for each schedule. It does not appear that the number of subjects is uniformly the factor of prime importance, or that such a ruling will meet the essential difficulty regarding failure. The failure in any subject will more often tend to indicate a specific difficulty rather than any general lack of 'ability plus application' relative to the number of subjects. The maladjustment is not so often in the size of the load as in the kind or composition of the load for the particular individual concerned. The burden is sometimes mastered by repeated trials. But often the particular adjustment needed is clearly indicated by the antecedent failures.

2. DISCONTINUANCE OF SUBJECT OR COURSE, AND THE SUBSTITUTION OF OTHERS

Earlier in this chapter appears the number and percentage of failures whose disposition was effected by discontinuance or by substitution. Twenty-four and five-tenths per cent of the failures were accounted for in this way. This grouping happens to be a rather complex one. Many of such pupils simply discontinue the course and then drop out of school. Some discontinue the subject but because they have extra credits take no substitute for it; others substitute in a general way to secure the needed credits but not specifically for the subject dropped. Only a few shift their credits to another curriculum. In some instances the subject is itself an extra one, and needs no substitute. For the graduating pupils only about 5 per cent of the failures are disposed of by discontinuing and by substitution of subjects. This fact may be due to the greater economy in examinations, or to the relatively inflexible school requirements for completing the prescribed work by repetition whether for graduation or for college entrance. In only one school was there a tendency to discontinue the subject failed in. So far as failures represent a definite maladjustment between the pupil and the school subject, the substitution of other work would seem to be the most rational solution of the difficulty.

A consideration of the success following a substitution of vocational or shop subjects, to replace the academic subjects of failure, offers an especially promising theme for study. No opportunity was offered in the scope of this study to include that sort of inquiry, but its possibilities are recognized and acknowledged herein as worthy of earnest attention. In only two of the eight schools was any shop-work offered, and only one of these could probably claim vocational rank. Apart from the difficulty in reference to comparability of standards, there were not more than a negligible number of cases of such substitution, due partly to the relative recency in the offering of any vocational work. In this reference a report comes from W. D. Lewis of an actual experiment[4] in which " fifty boys of the school loafer type . . . selected because of their prolific record in failure— as they had proved absolute failures in the traditional course— were placed in charge of a good red-blooded man in a thoroughly equipped wood work shop." " The shop failed to reach just one." At the same time the academic work improved. One cannot be sure of how much to credit the type of work and how much the red-blooded man for such results. But we may feel sure of further contributions of this sort in due time.

3. Employment of School Examinations

The school examinations employed to dispose of the failures are of two types. The ' final ' semester examination, employed by certain schools and required of pupils who have failed, operates to remove the previous failure for that semester of the subject. The success of this plan is not high, because of the insufficient time available to make any adequate reparation for the failures already charged. Of the 1,657 examinations of this kind to satisfy for failures, 30.7 per cent result in success. The boys are more successful than the girls by 4.5 per cent. This particular procedure is not employed by more than two of the eight schools. The other form of school examination employed for disposing of failures is the special examination, usually following some definite preparation, and given at the discretion of the teacher or department head. Its employment seems also to be limited pretty much to two of the schools, because for most of the subjects the Regents' examinations tend to displace it in the schools of the New York State and City systems. As only the successes were sure of being recorded in these tests we do not know the percentage of success attributable to this plan of removing failures. It 'probably deserves to be credited with a fairly high degree of success, for relatively few pupils (less than 200) utilize it, and then frequently after some extra preparation or study—such as summer school courses or tutoring. These two forms of school examinations jointly yield 37.5 per cent of successes on the number attempted, so far as such are recorded.

4. The Service Rendered by the Regents' Examinations in New York State

Whatever may be the merits or demerits of the Regents' examination system in general for academic school subjects, these tests certainly perform a saving function for the failing pupils, by promptly rectifying so many of their school failures and thus rescuing them from the burden of expensive repetition. A pupil's success in the Regents' examination has the immediate effect of satisfying the school failure charged to him. At the same time, it is possible, as is sometimes asserted, that the anticipation of these tests inclines some teachers to a more gratuitous distribution of failing marks as a spur to their pupils to brace up and perform well in reference to the Regents' questions. However, there is no trace of that policy found so far as the schools included in this study are concerned. For the three New Jersey schools considered jointly have a higher percentage of failing pupils, and a slightly higher average in the number of failures for each failing pupil than have the three New York State schools.

But it is more probable that the attitude referred to operates to exclude the failing pupils from being freely permitted to enter the Regents' tests in the failing subjects, and thus to restrain them from what threatens to lower the school percentage of successful papers, except that in New York City such discrimination is prohibited.[5] On the percentages of success for these examination results teachers and even schools are wont to be popularly judged. Annual school reports may feature the passing percentage for the school in Regents' examinations, with a spirit of pride or rivalry, but with no word of what that percentage costs as real cost must be reckoned. It is interesting to note in this connection that the percentage of unsuccessful repetitions for the three New Jersey schools is 13.7 per cent lower than for the three New York schools. In addition to this, for the latter schools 22 per cent more of the subject failures are repeated than for the former ones mentioned. It is important also to bear in mind that the success percentage for the Regents' tests is computed on the number admitted to the examinations—not on the number instructed in the subject. The regulations are flexible and admit of considerable latitude in matters of classification and interpretation. Accordingly, if it happens anywhere in the state that those who are the less promising candidates, in the teacher's judgment, are debarred from attempting Regents' examinations by failing marks, by demotion and exclusion from their class, or by other means, the school's percentage of pupils passing may be kept high as a result, but the injustice worked upon the pupil in such manner is vicious and reprehensible. Yet the whole intolerableness of the practice will center in the rule for exclusion of pupils from these examinations because of school failure. No one can predict with any safe degree of certainty that the outcome of any individual's efforts will be a failure in the Regents' tests, even though he has failed in a school subject. If failure should happen to result, it is chiefly the school pride that suffers; if the pupil is denied a free trial, he may suffer an injustice to aid the pretension of the school. Our school sanctions are not characterized by such acumen or infallibility as to warrant our refusing to give a pupil the benefit of the doubt. He is entitled to his chance to win success in these examinations if he is able, and it appears that only results in the Regents' tests can be truly trusted to tell us that he is or is not able to pass them.

The facts depicted here may lead to the belief that the recorded success in Regents' examinations may sometimes be artificially high, due to the subtle influences at work to make it so. In New York City absence is the sole condition for debarring any pupil, since he must have pursued a subject the prescribed time. Such a ruling is highly commendable, and it should not in fairness to the pupil be otherwise anywhere in the state. The following distribution discloses that 72.8 per cent of the 3,085 failing pupils who were recorded as taking the Regents' examinations were successful, and that 78 per cent of those succeeding passed in the same semester in which the school failure occurred.

SUCCESS OF THE FAILING PUPILS IN THE REGENTS' EXAMINATIONS

	Pass the Same Semester	Pass a Later Semester	Fail First, then Pass	Only Fail
1333 Boys..............	809	143	38	343
1752 Girls..............	946	193	117	496
Per Cent of Total.......		72.8		27.2

The divisions of the above distribution are distinct, with no overlapping or double counting. Of the pupils who pass these examinations in a later semester than that in which the failure occurs, a major part belong to the two schools which restrict their pupils mainly to a repetition of the subject after failing before they attempt the Regents' tests. Otherwise many of them would pass the Regents' examinations at once, as in the other schools, and would not need to repeat the subject. It was pointed out in the initial part of this chapter that 3.2 per cent of the instances of failure were followed by both repetition and examination. In one of the two schools referred to 90.8 per cent of the pupils failing and later taking Regents' examinations repeat the subject first. That most of such repetition is almost entirely needless is suggested by the fact that only 2.1 per cent more of their pupils pass, of the ones attempting, than of the total number reported above, and that too in spite of the loss of pupils' time and public money by such repetition. It may be, and doubtless is, true that an occasional omission occurs in recording the results after such tests have been taken, but, since it is the avowed policy of each school to have complete records for their own constant reference (excepting that the practice of the smallest of the five units was not to record the Regents' failures, and for this school they had to be estimated), the failing results would not be expected to be omitted more often than the successes, so that only the totals would be perceptibly affected by such errors.

One may rightly be permitted to speculate a bit here as to the most probable reaction of the pupil in regard to his respect for the school standards and for the judgment and opinion of his teacher, when he so readily and repeatedly passes the official state tests almost immediately after his school has classed his work as of failing quality. Perhaps it becomes easier for him to feel that failure is not a serious matter but an almost necessary incident that accompanies the expectations of the usual school course, just as gout is sometimes regarded as a mere contingency of ease and plenty. If such be true, and the evidence establishes a strong probability that it is, then it is not a helpful attitude to develop in the pupil nor one of benefit to the school and to society.

5. CONTINUATION OF SUBJECT WITHOUT REPETITION

A limited number of records were available in one school for the pupils who failed in the first semester of a subject, and who were permitted to continue the subject conditionally a second semester without first repeating it. Not all pupils were given this privilege, and the conditions of selection were not very definite beyond a sort of general confidence and promise relative to the pupil. The after-school conference was the only specific means provided for aiding such pupils. But 52 per cent of such subjects were passed in this manner, and the subsequent passing compensated for the previous failure as to school credit.

GRADES FOR FAILING PUPILS WHO CONTINUE THE SUBJECT WITHOUT REPETITION

	A	B	C	D
259 Boys	..	7	133	119
249 Girls	..	3	119	125
Per Cent of Total	..		52	48

A difference of judgments may prevail as to the significance of these facts. Although the passing grades secured are not high, 52 per cent have thus been relieved from the subject repetition, which on the average results in 33.3 per cent of failures, as has been noted in section 1 of this chapter.

A much more ingenious device for enabling at least some pupils to escape the repetition and yet to continue the subject was discovered in one school, in which it had been employed. Briefly stated, the scheme involved a nominal passing grade of

70 per cent, but a passing average of 75 per cent; and so long as the average was attained, the grade in one or two of the subjects might be permitted to drop as low as 60 per cent. Then in the event of a lower average than 75 per cent, it might be raised by a new test in the favorite or easiest subject, rather than in the low subject. By this scheme the grades could be so juggled as to escape repetition or other direct form of reparation in spite of repeated failures, unless perchance the grades fell below 60 per cent. By a change of administration in the school this whole scheme has been superseded. But it had been utilized to the extent that the records for this school showed practically no repetitions for the failing pupils.

A Summary of Chapter V

Among the school agencies for disposing of the failures, repetition of the subject is the most extensively employed.

Thirty-three and three-tenths per cent of the repeated grades are repeated failures.

Few of the repeaters take reduced schedules.

The repeaters with an extra schedule are more successful in each of the passing grades, and have 11.4 per cent less failures than repeaters with a normal or reduced schedule.

In the later subjects of the same kind, after failure and repetition, the unsuccessful grades are 2.2 per cent higher than for a similar situation without any repetition.

The grades in new work for repeaters are markedly superior to those in the repeated subjects, for the same semester.

As the number of identical repetitions are increased (as high as six), the percentage of final failure rapidly rises.

The emphasis placed on repetition is excessive, and the faith displayed in it by school practice is unwarranted by the facts.

Relatively few of the failing pupils who continue in school discontinue the subject or substitute another after failure.

School examinations are employed for 10.3 per cent of the failures, with 37.5 per cent of success on the attempts.

The Regents' examinations are employed for 17.2 per cent of the failures, of which 72.8 per cent succeed in passing, and in most cases immediately after the school failure.

Of those who continue the subject of failure without any repetition 52 per cent get passing grades.

No form of school compensation can be considered as adequate which does not adapt the treatment to the kind and cause of the malady, as manifested by the failure symptoms.

REFERENCES :

1. Briggs, T. H.   Report on Secondary Education, U. S. Comm. of Educ. Report, 1914.
2. Snedden, D.   In Johnson's *Modern High School.*   II, 24, 26.
3. Official Bulletin on Promotion and Students' Programs, 1917, from Assoc. Supt. in Charge of Secondary Schools, for N. Y. City.
4. Lewis, W. D.   *Democracy's High School,* p. 45.
5. Ruling of Board of Supt's., New York City, June, 1917.

CHAPTER VI

DO THE FAILURES REPRESENT A LACK OF CAPABIL-
ITY OR OF FITNESS FOR HIGH SCHOOL WORK
ON THE PART OF THOSE PUPILS?

In view of the fact that some of the pupils do not fail in any part of their school work, there is a certain popular presumption that failure must be significant of pupil inferiority when it occurs. That connotation will necessarily be correct if we are to judge the individual entirely by that part of his work in which he fails, and to assume that the failing mark is a fair indication of both achievement and ability. Although the pupil is only one of the contributing factors in the failure, nevertheless it happens that cherished opportunity, prizes, praise, honors, employment, and even social recognition are frequently proffered or withheld according to his marks in school. Still further, the pupil who accumulates failures may soon cease to be aggressively alive and active; he is in danger of acquiring a conforming attitude of tolerance toward the experience of being unsuccessful. Therefore it is particularly momentous to the pupil, should the school record ascribed to him prove frequently to be incongruous with his potential powers. It has already been pointed out in these pages that the failures frequently tend to designate specific difficulties rather than what is actually the negative of ' ability plus application.' This does not at all deny that in some instances there appears to be the ability minus the application, and that in other cases the pupils are simple unfitted for the work required of them.

1. Some Are Evidently Misfits

There is a strong presumption that many of the 485 pupils who failed in 50 per cent of their school work and dropped out (reported in Chapter IV) represent misfits for at least the kind of

76

school subjects offered or required. One cannot say that even hopeless failing in any particular subject is a safe criterion of general inability, or that failure in abstract sort of mental work would be a sure prophecy of failure in more concrete hand work. It is altogether probable that some of the individuals in the above number were not endowed to profit by an academic high school course, and that others were the restless ones at a restless age, who just would not fit in, whatever their abilities. But even of these pupils a considerable number display sufficient resourcefulness to satisfy many of their failures and to persist in school two, three, or four years. There are perhaps at least a few others who, without failing, drop out early, prompted by the conviction of their own unfitness to succeed in the high school. Yet collectively this group is by no means a large one. This conclusion is in harmony with the judgment of former Superintendent Maxwell, of New York City,[1] who stated that "the number of children leaving school because they have not the native ability to cope with high school studies, is, in my judgment, small." Likewise Van Denburg[2] reached the conclusion that "at least 75 per cent of the pupils who enter (high school) have the brains, the native ability to graduate, if they chose to apply themselves." With many who fail not even is the application lacking, as the facts of section 2 will seem to prove.

2. Most of the Failing Pupils Lack Neither Ability or Earnestness

When we take into account that by the processes of selection and elimination only thirty to forty per cent of the pupils who enter the elementary school ever reach high school,[3] it is readily admitted that the high school population is a selected group, of approximately 1 in 3. Then of this number we again select less than 1 in 3 to graduate. This gives a 1 in 9 selection, let us say, of the elementary school entrants. For relatively few general purposes in life may we expect to find so high a degree of selection. Yet in this 1 in 9 group (who graduate) the percentage of the failing pupils is as high as that of the non-failing ones, and the percentage of graduates does not drop even as the number of failures rise. So far as ability is required to meet the conditions of graduation they are manifestly provided with it. Following this comparison still further, the failing pupils who do not graduate have an average number of failures that is only .6 higher than for the failing graduates (4.9-4.3) ; but barring those non-graduates considered in section 1 of this chapter, the average is practically the same as for the failing graduates. Moreover, the failing non-graduates continue in school, even in the face of failure, much longer than do the non-failing non-graduates. That gives evidence of the same quality to which the manager of a New York business firm paid tribute when he said that he preferred to employ a high school graduate for the simple reason that the graduate had learned, by staying to graduate, how to 'stick to' a task.

The success of the failing pupils in passing the Regents' examinations does not give endorsement to the suggestion that they are in any true sense weaklings. That they succeed here almost concurrently with the failure in the school testifies that 'they can if they will,' or conversely, as regards the school subject, that 'they can but they won't.' Of course it is possible that differences in the type of examinations or in the standards of judgment as employed by the school and the Regents may be a factor in the difference of results secured. The great difficulty then seems to resolve itself into a technical problem of more successfully enlisting the energy and ability which they so irrefutably do possess in order to secure better school results, but perhaps in work that is better adapted to them. Again, the success with which these pupils carry a schedule of five or six subjects, besides other work not recognized in the treatment of this study, and retrieve themselves in the unattractive subjects of failure pleads for a recognition of their ability and enterprise. Their difficulty is without doubt frequently more physiological than psychological, except as they are the victims of a false psychology, that either disregards or misapplies the principles which Thorndike terms the law of readiness[4] to respond and the law of effect, and consequently depend largely on the one law of exercise of the function to secure the desired results.

Some additional evidence that the failing pupils can and do succeed in most of their subjects is provided by their earlier and later records, as disclosed by the total grades received for the semester first preceding and the one next following that in which the failure occurs. There were of course no preceding grades for the failures that occur in the first semester, and none succeeding those that occur in the last semester spent in school. It is quite apparent from the following distribution of grades that these pupils are far from helpless in regard to the ability required to do school work in general.

GRADES OF THE FAILING PUPILS IN THE SEMESTER NEXT PRECEDING THE FAILURES

Total	A	B	C	D
13,857 Boys	315	2883	6668	3991
17,264 Girls	245	2868	9509	4642
Per Cent of Total	1.8	18.5	52.0	27.7

GRADES OF THE FAILING PUPILS IN THE SEMESTER NEXT SUCCEEDING THE FAILURES

Total	A	B	C	D
14,724 Boys	319	2772	7406	4227
16,942 Girls	281	2788	9114	4759
Per Cent of Total	1.9	17.7	52.1	28.3

More than 20 per cent of the grades in the former and nearly 20 per cent of the grades in the latter distribution are A's or B's, 52 per cent more in each case are given a lower passing grade, while approximately 28 per cent in each distribution have failing grades. Though some tendency toward a continuity of failures is apparent, there is also evident a pronounced tendency in the main for pupils to succeed. That these same pupils could do better is not open to doubt. Teachers in two of the larger schools asserted that with many pupils a kind of complacency existed to feel satisfied with a C, and to consider greater effort for the sake of higher passing marks as a waste of time. Such pupils openly advocate a greater number of subjects with at least a minimum passing mark in each, in preference to fewer subjects and the higher grades, which they claim count no more in essential credit than a lower passing grade. That attitude may account for some of the low marks as well as for some of the failures shown above, even though the pupils may possess an abundance of mental ability.

Still another element, apart from the real ability of the pupils, which is contributory to school failures is found in punitive marking or in the giving of a failing grade for disciplinary effect. It is probably a relatively small element, but it is difficult to establish any certain estimate of its amount. Numerous teachers are ready to assert its reality in practice. Two cases came directly to the author's personal attention by mere chance —one, by the frank statement of a teacher who had used this weapon; another, by the ready advice of an older to a younger teacher, in the midst of recording marks, to fail a boy " because he was too fresh." The advice was followed. Such a practice, however prevalent, is intolerable and indefensible. If the school failure is to be administered as a retaliation or convenience by the teacher, how is the moral or educational welfare of the pupil to be served thereby? It is certain to be more efficacious for vengeance than for purposes of reforming the individual if employed in this way. The Regents' rules take recognition of this inclination toward a perversion of the function of examination by forbidding any exclusion from Regents' examinations as a means of discipline. Many teachers cultivate a finesse for discerning weaknesses and faults, without perceiving the immeasurable advantage of being able to see the pupils' excellences. In one school there was employed a plan by which a percentage discount was charged for absence, and in some instances it reduced a passing mark to a failing mark. This comes close to the assignment of marks of failure for penalizing purposes, which is unjustified and vicious.

It is certain that some of the pupils are failures only in the narrow academic sense. Information in reference to a few such cases was volunteered by principals, without any effort being made to trace such pupils in general. One of the pupils in this study who had graduated after failing 23 times, was able to enter a reputable college, and had reached the junior year at the time of this study. Two others with a record of more than 20 failures each had made a decided success in business—one as an automobile salesman and manager, the other in a telegraph office. It is not unrecognized that the school has many notable failures to indicate how even the fittest sometimes do not survive the school routine. Among such cases were Darwin, Beecher, Seward, Pasteur, Linnaeus, Webster, Edison, and George Eliot, who were classed by their schools as stupid or incompetent.[5]   In reference to the pupil's responsibility for the failures, Thorndike remarks[6] that "something in the mental or social and economic status of the pupil who enters high school, or in the particular kind of education given in the United States, is at fault. The fact that the elimination is so great in the first year of the high school gives evidence that a large share of the fault lies with the kind of education given in the United States." Some of the facts for those are not eliminated so early are still more definitely indicative that something is wrong with the kind of education given, as the facts of the following section seem to point out.

3. The School Emphasis and the School Failures Are Both Culminative in Particular School Subjects

As soon as we find any subject forced upon all pupils alike as a school requirement we may be quite sure that it will not meet the demands of the individual aptitudes and capacities of some portion of those pupils. As a result an accumulation of failures will tend to mark out such a uniformly required subject, whether it be mathematics, science or Latin. It was pointed out in section 4 of Chapter II that Latin and mathematics, although admittedly in charge of teachers ranking with the best, have both a high percentage of the total failures and the highest percentage of failures reckoned on the number taking the subject. In both regards there is a heaping up of failures for those two subjects, but furthermore there is an arbitrary emphasis culminating in these two subjects beyond any others excepting that English is a very generally required subject. In reference to these two required subjects the pupils who graduate are not more successful than those who do not. When the emphasis is on the teaching of the subject rather than on the teaching of the pupil there is no incongruity in making the subject a requirement for all, but both are incongruous with what psychology has more lately recognized and pointed out as to the wide range of individual differences. A similar situation is evidenced by the percentage of failure in science as reported for the St. Louis high school in Chapter II. A year of physics had been made compulsory for all, and taught in the second year.[7] Its percentage of failures accordingly mounts to the highest place. Mr. Meredith, who conducted that portion of the survey, rightly regards the policy as a mistake, and recommends that the needs of individual pupils be considered.

It is indeed striking how failures of the pupils are grouped under particular subjects of difficulty, and how the pupils fail again and again in the same general subject. No educational expert would seem to be needed to diagnose a goodly number of these chronic cases of failing and to detect a productive source of the whole trouble if only the following distribution were presented to him.

DISTRIBUTION OF PUPILS ACCORDING TO THE NUMBER OF TIMES THEY HAVE FAILED IN THE SAME SUBJECT

No. of Times	1	2	3	4	5	6	7	8	9	10	11	12	14
Boys.........	2852	1416	425	196	73	25	2	4	1	1	1	0	1
Girls.........	2812	1722	501	250	98	31	7	8	3	1	0	3	0

By 'same subjects' the same general divisions are designated, as English, Latin, mathematics. We may be led to note first that a major portion of the above distribution of pupils belongs to those who fail but once in the same subject; but then we note that by far the greater number of failures comprised by that distribution belong to those who fail two or more times in the same subject. To state that fact more specifically, 68.5 per cent of the total 17,960 failures involved in this study are made by two or more failures in the same subject, while 31.5 per cent of the failures belong to a more promiscuous and varied collection of failures, of not more than one in any subject. It will be noted here that some subjects do not have a greater continuity than one year or even one semester on the school program. Such subjects provide the least possibility of successive failures in the same field. A further analysis shows that the failures incurred by three or more instances occurring in the same subject form 33.6 per cent of the entire number; and that 18 per cent of the total is comprised of four or more instances of failure in the same subject. There is small probability that such a multiplication of failures by subjects will characterize the subjects which are least productive of failures in general, and such is not the case in fact. Latin and mathematics are again the chief contributors, and this would seem to be a fact also for those schools quoted from outside of this study, for purposes of comparison in Chapter II.

The above distribution speaks with graphic eloquence of how the school tends to focus emphasis on the subject prescribed and then to demand that the pupil be fitted or become fitted to the courses offered. Such heaping up of failures will more likely mark those subjects which seem to the pupil to be furthest from meeting his needs and appealing to his interests.

In two of the schools studied, an X, Y, and Z division was formed in certain difficult subjects for the failing pupils, by which they take three semesters to complete two. semesters of work. This plan, as judged by results, is obviously insufficient for such pupils and tends to prove further that the kind of work is more at fault in the matter of failing than is the amount. Frequently a pupil who fails in the A semester (first) will also fail in the X division of that subject as he repeats it, while at the same time his work is perhaps not inferior in the other subjects. The data for these special divisions were not kept distinct in transcribing the records, so that it is not possible to offer the tabulated facts here. There are numerous recognized illustrations of how some pupils find some particular subject as history, mathematics, or language distinctively difficult for them.

4. An Indictment Against the Subject-Matter and the Teaching Ends, as Factors in Producing Failures

The evidence already disclosed to the effect that the high school entrants are highly selected, that few of the failing pupils lack sufficient ability for the work, that they have manifested their ability and energy in diverse ways, and that particular subjects are unduly emphasized and by the uniformity of their requirement cause much maladjustment, largely contributing to the harvest of failures, seems to warrant an indictment against both the subject-matter and the teaching ends for factoring so prominently in the production of failures. There is clearly an administrative and curriculum problem involved here in the sense that not a few of the failures seem to represent the cost at which the machinery operates. This is in no sense intended as a challenge to any subject to defend its place in the high school curriculum, but it is meant to challenge the policy of the indiscriminate requirement of any subject for all pupils, allowing only that English of some kind will usually be a required subject for the great majority of the pupils. It is simply demanded that Latin and mathematics shall stand on their own merits, and that the same shall apply to history and science or other subjects of the curriculum. So far as they are taught each should be taught as earnestly and as efficiently as possible; but it should not be asked that any teacher take the responsibility for the unwilling and unfitted members of a class who are forced into the subject by an arbitrary ruling which regards neither the motive, the interest or the fitness of the individual.

This indictment extends likewise to the teaching method or purpose which focalizes the teachers' attention and energy chiefly on the subject. Certain basic assumptions, now pretty much discredited, have led to the avowed teaching of the subject for its own sake, and often without much regard to any definite social utility served by it. This charge seems to find an instance in the handling of the subject of English so that 16.5 per cent of all the failures are contributed by it, without giving even the graduate a mastery of direct, forceful speech, as is so generally testified. Strangely enough, except in the light of such teaching ends, the pupils who stay through the upper years and to graduate have more failures in certain subjects than the non-graduates who more generally escape the advanced classes of these subjects. The traditional standards of the high school simply do not meet the dominant needs of the pupils either in the subject-content or in the methods employed. Some of these traditional methods and studies are the means of working disappointment and probably of inculcating a genuine disgust rather than of furnishing a valuable kind of discipline. The school must provide more than a single treatment for all cases. In each subject there must be many kinds of treatment for the different cases in order to secure the largest growth of the individuals included. This does not in any sense necessitate the displacement of thoroughness by superficiality or trifling, but on the contrary greater thoroughness may be expected to result, as helpful adaptations of method and of matter give a meaningful and purposeful motive for that earnest application which thoroughness itself demands.

SUMMARY OF CHAPTER VI

The pupil is but one of several factors involved in the failure, yet the consequences are most momentous for him.

The pupils who lack native ability sufficient for the work are not a large number.

The high school graduates represent about a 1 in 9 selection of the elementary school entrants, but in this group is included as high a percentage of the failing pupils as of the non-failing ones.

The success of the failing pupils in the Regents' examinations, and also in their repeating with extra schedules, bears witness to their possession of ability and industry.

In the semester first preceding and that immediately subsequent to the failure, 72 per cent of all the grades are passing, 20 per cent are A's or B's. Many of them " can if they will."

The early elimination of pupils, the number that fail, and the notable cases of non-success in school are evidence of something wrong with the kind of education.

The characteristic culmination of failures for Latin and mathematics can hardly be considered a part of the pupils' responsibility.

Of all the failures 68.5 per cent are incurred by instances of two or more failures in the same subject.

Much maladjustment of the subject assignments is almost inevitable by a prescribed uniformity of the same content and the same treatment for all.

The traditional methods and emphasis probably account for more disappointment and disgust than for valuable discipline.

REFERENCES :

1. Maxwell, W. H. *A Quarter Century of Public School Development*, p. 88.
2. Van Denburg, J. K. *The Elimination of Pupils from Public Secondary Schools*, p. 183.
3. Annual Report of the U. S. Commissioner of Education, 1917.
4. Thorndike, E. L. *Educational Psychology*, Vol. II, Chap. I.
5. Swift, E. J. *Mind in the Making*, Chap. I.
6. Thorndike, E. L. *Elimination of Pupils from School*, U. S. Bull. 4, 1907.
7. Meredith, A. B. *Survey of the St. Louis Public Schools*, 1917, Vol. III, pp. 51, 40.

CHAPTER VII

WHAT TREATMENT IS SUGGESTED BY THE DIAGNOSIS OF THE FACTS OF FAILURE?

It is not the purpose of this chapter to formulate conclusions that are arbitrary, fixed, or all-complete. There are definite reasons why that should not be attempted. The author merely undertakes to apply certain well recognized and widely accepted principles of education and of psychology, as among the more important elements recommending themselves to him in any endeavor to derive an adequate solution for the situation disclosed in the preceding chapters. The significance of those preceding chapters in reference to the failures of the high school pupils is not at all conditioned by this final chapter. Since as a problem of research the findings have now been presented, it is possible that others may find the basis therein for additional or different conclusions from the ones suggested here. For such persons Chapter VII need not be considered an inseparable or essentially integral part of this report on the field of the research. Indeed the purpose of this study will not have been served most fully until it has been made the subject of dicussion and of criticism; and the treatment that is recommended here will not necessarily preclude other suggestions in the general effort to devise a solution or solutions that are the most satisfactory.

It appears from the analysis made in Chapter VI of the pupils' capability and fitness relative to the school failures that it is impossible to make any definite apportionment of responsibility to the pupils, until we have first frankly faced and made an effective disposition of the malfunctioning and misdirection as found in the school itself. It does not follow from this that any radical application of surgery need be recommended, but instead, a practical and extended course of treatment should be prescribed, which will have due regard for the nature and location of the ills to be remedied. Anything less than this will seem to be a mere external salve and leave untouched the chronic source of the systematic maladjustment. It is not assumed that a school system any more than any other institution or machine can be operated without some loss. But the failure of the school to make a natural born linguist pass in a subject of technical mathematics is perhaps unfortunate only in the thing attempted and in the uselessness of the effort.

We must take into account at the very beginning the fundamental truth stated by Thorndike,[1] that "achievement is a measure of ability only if the conditions are equal." Corollary to that is the fact that the same uniform conditions and requirements are often very unequal as applied to different individuals. The equalization of educational opportunity does not at all mean the same duplicated method or content for all. That interpretation will controvert the very spirit and purpose of the principle stated. Any inflexible scheme which attempts to fashion all children into types, according to preconceived notions, and whose perpetuity is rooted in a psychology based on the uniformity of the human mind, simply must give way to the newer conception which harmonizes with the psychic laws of the individual, or else continue to waste much time and energy in trying to force pupils to accomplish those things for which they have neither the capacity nor the inclination. It is accordingly obligatory on the school to give intelligent and responsive recognition to the wide differentiation of social demands, and to the extent and the continuity of the individual differences of pupils.

1. Organization and Adaptation in Recognition of the Individual Differences in Abilities and Interests

If the school failures are to be substantially reduced, the teaching of the school subjects with the chief emphasis on the pupil must surely replace the practice of teaching the subjects primarily for their own sake. This 'subject first' treatment must give place to the 'pupil first' idea. No subject then will overshadow the pupil's welfare, and the pupil will not be subjected to the subject. Education in terms of subject-matter is well designed to produce a large crop of failures. Neither the addition or subtraction of subjects is urged primarily, but the adaptation and utilization of the school agencies so as to make the pupils as efficient and as productive as possible, by recognizing first of all their essential lack of uniformity in reference to capacities and interests,—not only as between different individuals, but in the same individual at different ages, at different stages of maturity, and in different kinds of subjects. This conception precludes the school employment of subjects and methods for all alike which are obviously better adapted to the younger than to the older. Neither does it overlook the fact that the attitude of more mature pupils toward authority and discipline is essentialy different from that of the younger boys and girls; that a subject congenial to some pupils will be intolerable and nearly if not quite impossible for others; or that an appeal designed mainly to reach the girls will not reach boys equally well. In brief, the treatment proposed here is neither radical nor novel, but it is simply the institution of applied psychology as pertaining to school procedure. What the more modern experimental psychology has established must be utilized in the school, at the expense of the more obsolete and traditional. Psychology now generally recognizes the existence of what the general school procedure implies does not exist, namely, the wide range of individual differences.

The situation clearly demands that our public schools shall not, by clinging to precedent and convention, fall notably behind industry and government in appropriating the fruits of modern scientific research. As the doctor varies the diet to the needs of each patient and each affliction, so must the school serve the intellectual and social needs of the pupils by such an organization and attitude that the selection of subjects for each pupil may take an actual and specific regard of the individual to be served. The change all important is not necessarily in the school subject or curriculum, but rather a change in the attitude as to how a subject shall be presented—to whom and by whom. The latter will also determine the character of the pupil's response and the subject's educational value to him. By securing a genuine response from the pupils a subject or course of study is thereby translated into pupil achievement and human results. The authority of the school is impotent to get these results by merely commanding them or by requiring all to pursue the same subject. An experience, in order to have truly educational value, must come within the range of the pupils comprehension and interest. Quoting Newman,[2] " To get the most out of an experience there must be more or less understanding of its better possibilities. The social and ethical implications must somewhere and at some time be lifted very definitely into conscious understanding and volition." The pupil's responsiveness is then much more important both for securing results and for reducing failures than is any subject content or method that is not effective in securing a tolerable and satisfying sort of mental activity.

2. FACULTY STUDENT ADVISERS FROM THE TIME OF ENTRANCE

Not only the failure of pupils in their school subjects but the failure also of 13 per cent of them to remain in school even to the end of the first semester, or of 23.1 per cent to remain beyond the first semester (Tables V and VI)—of whom a relatively small number had failed (about ¼)—make a strong appeal for the appointment of sympathetic and helpful teachers as student advisers from the very time of their entrance. One teacher is able to provide personal advice and educational guidance for from 20 to 30 pupils. The right type of teachers, their early appointment, and the keeping of some sort of confidential and unofficial record, all seem highly important.

Superintendent Maxwell mentioned among the reasons why pupils leave school[3] that " they become bewildered, sometimes scared, by the strange school atmosphere and the aloofness of the high school teachers." There is a strangeness that is found in the transition to high school surroundings and to high school work which certainly should not be augmented by any further handicap for the pupil. There are no fixed limitations to what helpfulness the advisers may render in the way of ' a big brother ' or ' big sister ' capacity. It is all incidental and supplementary in form, but of inestimable value to the pupils and the school. A further service that is far more unusual than difficult may be performed by the pupils who are not new, in the way of removing strangeness for those who are entering what seems to them a sort of new esoteric cult in the high school. The girls of the Washington Irving High School[2] of New York City recently put into practice a plan to give a personal welcome to each entering girl, and a personal escort for the first hour, including the registration and a tour of the building, in addition to some friendly inquiries, suggestions, and introductions. The pupil is then more at home in meeting the teachers later. Here is the sort of courtesy introduced into the school that commercial and business houses have learned to practice to avoid the loss of either present or prospective customers. Some day the school must learn more fully that the faith cure is much cheaper than surgery and less painful as well.

3. Greater Flexibility and Differentiation Required

The recognition of individual differences urged in section 1 necessitates a differentiation and a flexibility of the high school curriculum that is limited only by the social and individual needs to be served, the size of the school, and the availability of means. The rigid inflexibility of the inherited course of study has contributed perhaps more than its full share to the waste product of the educational machinery. The importance of this change from compulsion and rigidity toward greater flexibility has already received attention and commendation. One authority[4] states that " one main cause of (H. S.) elimination is incapacity for and lack of interest in the sort of intellectual work demanded by the present courses of study," and further that " specialization of instruction for different pupils within one class is needed as well as specialization of the curriculum for different classes." There must be less of the assumption that the pupils are made for the schools, whose regime they must fit or else fail repeatedly where they do not fit. Theoretically considerable progress has already been made in the differentiation of curricula, but in practice the opportunity that is offered to the pupils to profit thereby is curtailed, because of the rigid organization of courses and the uniform requirements that are dictated by administrative convenience or by the college entrance needs of the minority. The only permissible limitations to the variables of the curriculum should be such as aim to secure a reasonable continuity and sequence of subjects in one or more of the fields selected. One of the chief barriers to a more general flexibility has been the notion of inequality between the classical and all other types of education. This assumption has had its foundations heavily shaken of late. The quality of response which it elicits has come to receive a precedence over the name by which a subject happens to be classified. " France has come out boldly and recognized at least officially the exact parity between the scientific education and the classical education." [5] Indeed one may doubt whether this parity will ever again be seriously questioned, because of the elevation of scientific training and accomplishment in the great world war, as well as in its adaptation for the direct and purposeful dealing with the problems of modern life. Especially for the early classes in the high school does the situation demand a relatively flexible curriculum, else the only choice will be to drop out to escape drudgery or failure. Inglis maintains that the selective function of the high school may operate by a process of differentiation rather than by a wholesale elimination.[6] The pupil surely cannot know in advance what he is best fitted for, but the school must help him find that out, if it is to render a very valuable service, and one at all comparable to the success of the industrial expert in utilizing his material and in minimizing waste. The junior high school especially aims to perform this function that is so slighted in the senior high school. Yet neither the organization nor the purpose of the two are so far apart as to excuse the helplessness of the latter in this important duty.

There is apparently no constitutional impediment to a still further extension of the principle of flexibility and to the minimizing of loss by what has been a costly trial and error method of fitting the pupils and the subjects to each other. Short unit courses are not unfamiliar in certain educational fields, and they lend themselves very readily to definite and specific needs. Their usefulness may be regarded as a warrant of a wider adoption of them. Although they are as yet employed mainly for an intensive form of training or instruction to meet specific needs of a particular group in a limited time,[7] the principle of their use is no longer novel. A unit course of an extensive nature is also conceivable, for instance, a semester of any subject entitled to two credits might allow a division into two approximately equal portions. If then both teacher and pupil feel, when one unit is completed, that the pupil is in the wrong subject or that his work is hopeless in that subject, he might be permitted to withdraw and be charged with a failure of only one point, that is, just one-half the failure of a semester's work in the subject—or one-fourth that for a whole year with no semester divisions. Even if this scheme would not work equally well in all subjects, it implies no extensive reorganization to employ it in the ones adapted. It is not incredible that, as the people more generally understand that physics, chemistry, and biology have become vital to national self-preservation and social well-being, their emphasis as subjects required or as subjects sought by most of the pupils may lead to a high percentage of failures, such as is found for Latin and mathematics usually, or for science as reported in St. Louis, where it was required of all and yielded the highest percentage of failures. Now the teaching of most sciences by the unit plan will comprise no greater difficulty than is involved in overcoming text-book methods and the conservatism of convention. The project device, as employed in vocational education, will also lend itself in many instances to the unit division of work. The first consequence of this plan will be a reduction of failures for the pupil in those subjects whose continued pursuit would mean increased failure. The second consequence may be to relieve teachers of hopeless cases of misfit in any subject, for if the pupils no longer have intolerable subjects imposed on them the teachers will come to demand only tolerable work in the subjects of their choice. The third consequence will probably be to encourage pupils to find themselves by trying out subjects at less risk of such cumulative failures as are disclosed in section 3 of the preceding chapter.

4. PROVISION FOR THE DIRECTION OF THE PUPILS' STUDY

The forms of treatment suggested in the first three sections of this chapter for the diminution of failures will find their natural culmination of effectiveness in a plan for helping the pupils to help themselves. This has been notably lacking in most school practice. Every improvement of the school adaptation still assumes that the pupils are to apply themselves to honest, thorough study. But the high school must bear in mind that good studying implies good teaching. It cannot be trusted to intuition or to individual discovery. Real, earnest studying is hard work. The teachers have usually presupposed habits of study on the part of the pupils, but one of the important lessons for the school to teach the pupil is how to use his mind and his books effectively and efficiently. Even the simplest kinds of apprenticeship instruct the novice in the use of each device and in the handling of each tool to a degree which the school most often disregards when requiring the pupil to use even highly abstract and complex instrumentalities. The practice of the school almost glorifies drudgery as a genuine virtue. E. R. Breslich refers to this fact,[8] saying, " so it happens that the preparation for the classwork, not the classwork itself burdens the lives of the pupils." The indefensibleness of the indiscriminate lesson giving consists in the fact that it is not the load but the harness that is too heavy. The harness is more exhausting and burdensome than the load appointed. The destination sought and the course to be followed in the lesson preparation are very many times not clearly indicated, lest the discipline, negative and repressive though it be, should be extracted from the struggle. The fact is that discouragement and failure are too often the best of testimony that teachers are not much concerned about how the pupil employs his time or books in studying a lesson. The point is illustrated admirably by the report in the *Ladies Home Journal,* for January, 1913, of a request from a hardworking widow that the teacher of one of her children in school try teaching the child instead of just hearing the lessons which the mother had taught.

Directing the pupils' study is sometimes regarded as a more or less formalized scheme of organization and procedure, which requires extra time, extra teachers, and a lesser degree of independence on the part of the pupils. But here too the important things are differentiation and specific direction as adapted to the needs of the subject, the topic or the pupils. It must be insisted that supervised study is not the same thing in all schools, in all subjects, or for all pupils. In other words, its very purpose is defeated if it is overformalized. An experiment is reported by J. H. Minnick with two classes in plane geometry,[9] of practically the same size, ability, and time allowance for study, which indicated that the supervised pupils were the less dependent as judged by their success in tests consisting of new problems. The pupils also liked the method, in spite of their early opposition, and no one failed, while two of the unsupervised class

failed.   William Wiener also speaks of the wonderful self-
control which springs from the supervised study program.[10]
As to the need of extra teachers for the purpose there is not
much real agreement, since the plans of adaptaion are so different in themselves.   Increased labor for the same teachers will
rightly imply greater renumeration.   Colvin makes mention
of the additional expense imposed by the larger force of teachers
required.[11]   But J. S. Brown finds that the failures are so
largely reduced that with fewer repeaters there is a consequent
saving in the teaching force.[12]   With a faculty of 66 teachers,
he reports 38 classes in which there was no failure, and a marked
reduction of failures in general by the use of supervised study.
It is interesting and significant to note here that by allowing 100
daily pupil recitations to the teacher the repeated subjects reported in this study would require 87 teachers for one semester
or 11 teachers for the full four years.   This fact represents
more than $50,000 in salaries alone.   Buildings, equipment, heat,
and other expenses will more than double the amount.   But
such expense is incomparable with what the pupils pay in time,
in struggles, and in disappointment in order to succeed later
in only 66.7 per cent of the subjects repeated.   As none of the
eight schools provided anything more definite than a general
after school hour for offering help, and which often has a punitive suggestion to it, the possibility of saving many of these
pupils from failure and repetition by the wise and helpful direction of their study is simply unmeasured.   A conclusion that is
particularly encouraging is reported by W. C. Reavis to the effect
that the poorer pupils—the ones who most need the direction—
are the ones that supervised study helps the most.[13]   There is
nothing novel in saying that good teaching and good studying
are but different aspects of the same process, but it would be
an innovation to find this conception generally realized in the
school practice.

5. A Greater Recognition and Exposition of the Facts As
Revealed by Accurate and Complete School Records

It is unfortunate that the detailed and complete records which
tell the whole story about the failures in the school and for
the individual are found in relatively few schools, even when

on all sides business enterprises find a complete system of detailed records, filed and indexed, altogether indispensable for their intelligent operation and administration. The school still proceeds in its sphere too much by chance and faith, forgetting mistakes and recalling successes. This is possible because there is no question of self-support or of solvency to face, and because neither the teachers nor the institution are in danger of direct financial loss by their waste, duplication, or failures. In the absence of records it is always possible to calmly assume that the facts are not so bad as for other schools which do report their recorded facts. The prevailing unfamiliarity with statistical methods may also favor a skepticism as to their proper application to education, since it is not an exact science. But the fact remains established that it is always possible to measure qualitative differences if stated in terms of their quantitative amounts.

Admirable and complete as are the records for the many schools of the minority group possessing them, their more general value and information are still quite securely hidden away in the files which contain them. Peculiarly interesting was the surprise expressed by the principals at the extensive and significant information which their own school records provided, when they received individual reports on the data collected and tabulated for this study. Yet they received only the portions of the tabulations which seemed most likely to interest them. The principals do not have the time or the assistance to study in a collective way the facts which are provided by their own records, but they are entitled to much credit for so courteously co-operating with any competent person for utilizing their records for approved purposes and in turn sharing their results with the school. To proceed wisely in the administration of the school we must have a chance to know and discuss the facts. It is not possible to know the facts without adequate records. The absence of evidence gives prominence to opinion and precedent. Accordingly, it is entirely incredible that the number, the repetition, and the accumulation of failures would remain unchanged after a fair exposition and discussion of the evidence presented in a collective and comprehensive form. It may be necessary to admit that a few teachers will hold opinions so strong that they will discredit all testimony not in support of such opinions. But the high school teachers in general seem fairly and earnestly disposed, even about revising their notions concerning the truth in any situation. In regard to the relative number and time of the failures, the actual and relative success in repeated work, the advantage of repetition for later work, the relation of success to the size of the schedule, the influence of the number of failures on graduation, and numbers of other vital facts, it could be said of the teachers in general that they simply knew not what they were doing. They even thought they were doing what they were not. The school records must be disclosed and utilized more fully if their value and importance are to be realized. It will be a large source of satisfaction if this report helps to direct attention to the official school records, from which a frequent ' trial balance ' will help to rectify and clarify the school practice. Both are needed.

Summary of Chapter VII

The contributing factors found in the school must first be remedied, before responsibility for the failures can be fairly apportioned to the pupils.

The provision of uniform conditions for all is based on the false doctrine of the uniformity of the human mind. Such conditions may prove very unequal for some individuals, and achievement is not then a real measure of ability.

By applying a functioning psychology to school practice, more adaptation and specialization are required to meet the individual differences of pupils.

No change of subjects is in general necessitated, but a change of the attitude which subjects pupils to the subjects seems essential.

The genuineness of the pupil's response depends on the pupil and the subject. A policy of coercion will usually beget only dislike or failure.

Properly selected student advisers, appointed early, may transform the school for the pupil, save the pupil for the school, and his work from failures.

A relatively high degree of flexibility and specialization of the curriculum will help the pupil find what he is best fitted for, and thereby minimize waste. This will include a virtual parity between the classical and scientific subjects.

The reduction of some subjects to smaller units will tend to facilitate flexibility and a reduction of failures.

The provision of directed study will help the pupils to help themselves. Good teaching demands it. The harness is often heavier than the load. Failures are inevitable.

The plan of study direction must be varied according to the varying needs of pupils, subjects, and schools. The poorer pupils are aided most. They are made even more reliant on themselves. The reduction of failures tends to balance any added expense.

Records adequate and complete should be a part of the business and educational equipment of every school. The exposition and use of these facts as recorded will then give direction to school progress, and dethrone the authority of assumption and opinion.

REFERENCES:

1. Thorndike, E. L. *Individuality*, pp. 38, 51.
2. Neuman, H. *Moral Values in Secondary Education*, United States Bureau of Education Bulletin, No. 51, 1917, pp. 18, 17.
3. Maxwell, W. H. *A Quarter Century of Public School Development*, p. 89.
4. Thorndike, E. L. *The Elimination of Pupils from School*, U. S. Bureau of Education Bulletin, No. 4, 1907, p. 10.
5. Farrington, F. E. *French Secondary Schools*, p. 124.
6. Inglis, A. *Principles of Secondary Education*, p. 669.
7. Committee of N. E. A. *Vocational Secondary Education*, U. S. Bureau of Education Bulletin No. 21, 1916, p. 58.
8. Breslich, E. R. *Supervised Study as Supplementary Instruction, Thirteenth Yearbook*, p. 43.
9 Minnick, J. H. "The Supervised Study of Mathematics," *School Review*, 21-670.
10. Wiener, W. "Home Study Reform," *School Review*, 20-526.
11. Colvin, S. S. *An Introduction to High School Teaching*, p. 366.
12. Brown, J. S. *School and Home Education*, February, 1915, p. 207.
13. Reavis, W. C. "Supervised Study," in Parker's *Methods of Teaching in the High School*, p. 398.